362.109728
N42e

A NEW DAWN
IN GUATEMALA

Toward a Worldwide Health Vision

Edited by

Richard Luecke

D1366793

WAVELAND
PRESS, INC.
Prospect Heights, Illinois

For information about this book, write or call:

Waveland Press, Inc.
P.O. Box 400
Prospect Heights, Illinois 60070
708/634-0081

Photographs by Ulli Steltzer. Copyright © 1983 by Ulli Steltzer.

A NEW DAWN
IN GUATEMALA

FUNDACIÓN GUATEMALTECA PARA EL DESARROLLO "CARROLL BEHRHORST" was incorporated in 1981 as a Guatemalan not-for-profit organization responsible for the Chimaltenango based program of health and development founded by Carroll Behrhorst in 1962. This fulfilled a founding objective that the Guatemala program should be led and controlled by Guatemalans.

THE BEHRHORST CLINIC FOUNDATION, INC., incorporated in New York in 1967, is an instrument of financial support and educational outreach for the Chimaltenago program.

A Partnership Agreement, signed in 1991, provides for cooperation between the boards in Chimaltenango and New York. Each has a voice and vote in the other's meetings and there is consultation with respect to major decisions. Working together, these boards afford a unique opportunity for individuals and associations in North America to achieve constructive interaction with people of the Guatemalan highlands and to make effective contributions to their efforts. Information may be obtained by writing or phoning either of these offices.

Fundación Guatemalteca para
el Desarrollo "Carroll Behrhorst"
Apartado Postal 15
Chimaltenango, Guatemala
Telephone: 391-356

The Behrhorst Clinic Foundation, Inc.
P.O. Box 1815
New York, New York 10009
Phone/Fax: (203) 846-0043

Carroll Behrhorst was a "healer" of many extreme schisms: between the science of medicine and the art of medicine, between medicine and health, between prevention and cure, between health and development, between professionals and people, between people's dependency and people's self-reliance, between passive community participation and active community involvement, between science and faith, between sympathy and empathy, and many others.

The health world drew heavily on many facets of work among the Maya in Guatemala when it unanimously accepted the Alma-Ata Declaration and Report on Primary Health Care in 1978 and when it adopted a worldwide goal of "Health for All by the Year 2000." In spite of skepticism and cynicism, primary health, in the best sense of love for people and life, has become a watershed in health thinking and increasingly in health practice.

Halfdan Mahler
Director General Emeritus, World Health Organization

CONTENTS

LEARNINGS FOR HEALTH CARE AROUND THE WORLD

A NEW DAWN
WITH FINGERS TO THE WORLD

Richard Luecke

Carroll Behrhorst died in Chimaltenango in May 1990 and was carried on shoulders of the Kaqchikel to a long-chosen burial site in Chimazat, the birthplace of his wife, Alicia Nicolás de Behrhorst. The customary words were spoken and many more words were added in both Spanish and Mayan tongues. For the people present this was also a familiar deed—like holding a grain of corn in one's hand and then laying it in the ground to wait for the sun. Nine days later and again a year later they were back to celebrate new life coming from the old.

On the walls of the Behrhorst complex in Chimaltenango has always hung the *amanecer* glyph—a Mayan symbol of the sunrise with its connotations of darkness and light, sleep and waking, imperception and sight, growth and cultivation, time and life, healing and divinity. The last of many organizations fostered by this doctor was composed of Maya-Kaqchikel workers calling themselves *Nuevo Amanecer*, "New Dawn," by way of declaring that what they had begun with the doctor would continue in his absence—in those days it was absences for teaching at the Tulane University School of Public Health and Tropical Medicine.

Among the many greetings flung around the world by Behrhorst through the years was one which copied out a sentence from Henry David Thoreau: "Only that day dawns to which we are awake." All this helps explain the title and the purpose of the papers gathered in this book. They seek to alert people to a new dawn of health activity which this doctor awaited and witnessed in Guatemala and reissue his invitation to join, in appropriate ways, the amanecer people.

Memories of Doc are always graphic—a crumpled jacket, stuffed briefcase, roundish shape. They are also audible—there was a twang, bounce and jubilance in his speech and a straightforward vocabulary which took back bodily functions from the medical Latin. Also attitudinal—he had no desire whatever to be an Albert Schweitzer or what he called a "white knight." And actional—a way of doing things that was at once self-directed and attentive to others, whether he was playing with children in the market, treating a hundred patients in a single long morning with no sense of haste, pulling teeth for a parade of quiet sufferers or driving with disciplined madness to a mountain village.

North American audiences who heard Behrhorst speak and later published his words from transcriptions sometimes expressed disappointment over the result. While the papers were still very valuable, you really had to be there. No more than the Mayan woman who stooped at his body during the internment crying for it to rise up («¡Levántate! Doctor, ¡levántate!») are we able to raise up the focal character of this book for the eyes and ears of its readers.

Contributors to this volume who had worked with Behrhorst in Chimaltenango invariably wished to describe bone-crushing rides in his jeep—splashing through water at the bottom of ravines amid the colors and arm waiving of launderers, then jolting upward to spectacular mountain vistas—a valid desire since the doctor himself loved those drives and that's when he talked most freely to visitors. We have, however, limited those rides to two and will take the first of these in the introduction by a North American physician—one who is now engaged in citizen-based reform of health policies and practices.

A novelist who took this ride became a leading spirit of the first Behrhorst support board in North America and wrote an earlier introduction called "The Man and His Ideas" (Knebel 1976).[1] That physician-novelist connection was no accident. While waiting to enter medical school at Washington University in St. Louis, a younger Carroll Behrhorst had devoured novel after novel. This literary appetite helps account for the references sprinkled through his writings to sources as different as Terrence, Walt Whitman and V.S. Naipaul and for the broader sensibilities which characterized his life's work. Cultural factors, though a very different sort, made the Chimaltenango program what it is.

LIGHT FROM THE KAQCHIKEL

The first three chapters in this book are from Mayan spokes-persons, all Kaqchikel, who belong to one of more than twenty dialect groups in Guatemala and speak one of four languages most widely used. The first contribution is by an extension worker and nurse of the program who describes early years during which she and residents of the villages taught the doctor what he needed to know and do in order to move among them and learn their ways.

The second Mayan voice is that of a native of Chimaltenango who is now president of the International Mayan League with offices in Costa Rica. We did not ask her to set forth the profound wisdom of the sacred books of the Maya which has been preserved, in spite of book burnings by conquerors, in the teachings of the elders. Nor did we ask for folkloric tales or rituals, though we knew the words she chose would have these behind them. Rather, we asked for a partial translation in general terms of Mayan understandings of health as they are carried day by day in the minds and habits of the villagers with whom the

---

[1]References in the Foreword are to be found in Bibliography and Resources, pp. 235ff.

Behrhorst program collaborates. What she describes is not to be viewed as "primitive" or "archaic" but as current and functioning.

The third of these papers was read in the Chimaltenango square by a leader of the Nuevo Amanecer workers on the occasion of the doctor's death. Its purpose was, first, to review their work during previous decades (this afforded a ritual for the hearers and offers a chronology to the readers) and then to secure a vow from all present that the cultural understandings and the goal of self-determination which had shaped their work in the past would always do so in the future. The speaker is now a vice-president of the foundation board in Guatemala. A final chapter to this entire volume is by the present foundation president in Chimaltenango who began work 30 years ago as a health promoter. Almost all the local board members at this time are Kaqchikel and they are fully aware that their teaching function must continue.

One of the points made by these spokespersons is that some creative combination seems possible between Mayan healing and "Western" medicine. Through the centuries the Maya have been ingenious grafters on ancient roots, as their very survival in large numbers attests. Somewhere in these papers we learn of Carroll Behrhorst's admiration of the great ceiba, a silk-cotton tree of Guatemala. This tree was depicted on the walls of Mayan temples many centuries before Columbus and is still to be seen, for example, in the temple of the foliated cross at Palenque in Chiapas, Mexico, dedicated in the year 690 on our calendar (Wright 1989:12, Canby 1992:50). It can also be seen in churches of Guatemala—for example, at the top of the altar piece at Santiago Atitlán in Sololá. Mayan women are proud to discover that the cross they embroider on their blouses derives from their own forebears and not simply, as they are sometimes taught, from their conquerors. In fact, the entire design of these blouses is a cross, with a sun at the center, through which the head emerges as from a tree.

This is a leafy cross whose roots, trunk and foliage are seen as uniting underworld, world and firmament. Laid flat, it represents the eye of God pointing the world's four directions. The people view themselves with other creatures as branches, leaves and sprouts of this world tree. They have a saying that, though their fruits have been plucked, their foliage cut back and their trunk

Grain pours through the hands at Simajuleu, a village whose name means "edge of the world." From here one sees the rest of the world as for the first time.

burned by invaders, their roots are still alive and able to send shoots through the layers of foreign soil deposited above them. All this partly explains the readiness and devotion with which many of the Maya came to adopt the Christian cross and also how they came to find in it an enriched understanding on their own. They could come similarly to an adopted and enriched understanding of the caduceus.

Such learning goes both ways. Behrhorst often said that he had gained much more from his Mayan friends than they had gained from him. People in the United States, he observed, tend to perceive health as the absence of pain or of any name disease. The people of Chimaltenango see health as the performance of positive functions: a good appetite, hard work, enjoyment of nature and participation in the village. Such functions combine aspects of life distinguished elsewhere as those of body, soul and spirit. Thus, health problems among the Maya extend beyond those of access to medical services and self-care to questions about human relationships with the rest of nature and with one another in community. The solutions, in which everyone is involved and in which ritual is important, include restoration, maintenance and promotion of health.

The photographs included in this book give readers the advantage of the appreciative and discerning eye of an experienced social photographer who devoted two extended sojourns to preparing a faithful pictorial and oral record of the Chimaltenango program (Steltzer 1983). She did not, as in one critical description of the modern camera, "barge in, stare and walk out." The reader is invited to pause over the faces of health promoters who are now among the many who have been slain or have "disappeared" in Guatamala, who are untimely and improperly "sown."

A DOCTOR WHO WORKED IN THAT LIGHT

Carroll Behrhorst customarily began his talks, lectures and newsletters by saying, "First, a little story from Chimaltenango." We've included a selection of these in the first of five chapters devoted to his own papers. Next is the doctor's own description of the Chimaltenango Development Program, one that grew through the years with major stopping places in a book published by the World Health Organization entitled *Health by the People* (Newell 1975) and in *Health in the Guatemalan Highlands* (Steltzer 1983). Here the reader will find an introduction to the various elements of the Chimaltenango program which are referred to in other papers: the specially formed clinic and hospital, health promoters, agricultural extension, land loans and reacquisition, women's programs and water programs along with commentary which capsulizes the first twenty years of working and learning with the people.

Two chapters follow which describe the role of this small highland program during events that shook, fascinated and horrified the world. These are not finished papers but a sequence of communications from the doctor during those fateful periods. Scenes of the devastation wrought by the earthquakes of 1976 were brought by television to living rooms in other hemispheres. A network radio commentator told listeners in the United States that the response of the Behrhorst program in this crisis was "an experience too durable for time to dissolve and too heart-tugging to neglect" (Morgan 1976-1980). A senior international health official in Guatemala wrote that "in this emergency Behrhorst had the best organized medical team in the country" (Heggenhougen 1976:Appendix X). When mail resumed, the doctor wrote to concerned friends and supporters that his family and the program were "in excellent straits." There was an unprecedented infusion of funds at this time, including larger amounts from religious, ecumenical and voluntary agencies, which helped rebuild physical facilities. But millions were also declined with the explanation, "We will accept money as we can properly use it."

The other crisis, watched by a horrified world, was the escalation of violence that marked the years following the fraudulent national election of 1978 and the fire bombing of protesting demonstrators in the Spanish embassy in 1980. A counterinsurgency offensive began in Chimaltenango and during the resulting civil warfare more than 400 highland villages were destroyed, leaving more than 50,000 widows and 150,000 orphans. In 1980 there were 313 registered non-governmental organizations working in the Department of Chimaltenango. By September 1982, all but 13 had left the scene in fear or protest and the Behrhorst program was one of two still functioning.

The policy of the local foundation was formed amid the turbulence of daily events. The local board formulated an official nonpolitical position and this was announced personally by the doctor to leaders on both sides. Such a nonaligned stance was severely criticized by some observers as reactionary and was viewed by some others as naive. (Behrhorst himself described in a communication how thin the line can become between health promotion and political initiatives for justice.) Still others have seen the Guatemalan foundation's policy as "naive like a fox," for the very survival of the program can be attributed to those communications delivered personally to both sides.

It is possible to point in justification of this middle-of-the-road policy to the physician's explicit vocation to "do no harm." It may be added that Behrhorst found those Maya with whom he lived and worked (including his wife, Alicia) opposed to violence by their cultural and religious formation; nor were they moving up to leadership in any armed groups. His own formation disposed him to nurse hopes for the powers that be, or for those that were next to be, and for civil restraint of regional military authorities. Yet to the end of his life the doctor was haunted by the dread pos-sibility—in fact, tragic reality—that the local foundation had left conscientious workers in the villages overexposed and under-protected.

There was from the beginning an announced readiness on the part of the foundation to respect and materially support any health promoters and villages that chose to continue their community organizing activities in spite of warnings or that chose to begin again after the threatenings and slaughters had taken place. From beginning to end (certainly from his 1975 essay), the doctor saw "integral development" as a long-term, patient process which must precede, accompany and outlast any effort toward a swift resolution of long injustice. A revolutionary Guatemalan poet wrote from exile in 1980 that the people should get up early to set forward the sunrise (*«para adelantar el amanecer»* — Julia Esquivel), an idea which has some basis in Mayan ritual and sacrificial invocations of the sun. But Behrhorst was impressed by the sense in which you can't "say to the dawn 'be soon'" (Francis Thompson). In the interest of *that* dawn he sometimes skipped the poetry and said brusquely, "It is very important to stay alive!"

These selected papers from the earthquake and the violence should, at the very least, convey real experiences and recent case studies that are "too durable for time to dissolve." We foresee long conversations among students or trainees who are considering work in countries other than their own. Two additional Behrhorst papers are included: one is an address to medical students in the United States and the other gathers up reflections on "primary health care" from his lectures and class notes at Tulane. A certain distance in time and space is not in every sense a disadvantage. North American readers may be surprised by an unpolished and striking relevance to the current discussion of public provisions and expenditures for health.

Other speeches and writings by Behrhorst are listed in the Chimaltenango bibliography at the end of this book. In *Voz del Pueblo*, a monthly paper from San Juan Comalapa, the doctor wrote regular columns on self-care and mutual care in cases of cough, fever, vomiting, diarrhea, rash, shortness of breath, back ache, ear ache and rheumatism along with strategies for addressing problems of home agriculture and small animal husbandry.

During the 1960s Behrhorst prepared advisory papers for the Lutheran mission board which first drew him to Guatemala and for related Guatemalan and Caribbean working groups. During the 1970s he made visits on behalf of medical mission boards to stations in Africa, Asia, Haiti and New Guinea and wrote extensive—often hilarious—reports. To friends he complained about "the bland Protestant food and the loss of his usual ration of wine" within the compounds. In Asia and Africa he found medical mission hospitals "doing a fine job within the compound walls—and an equally poor job outside those walls." In Papua, New Guinea, he agreed with the minister of health that the people "could not afford the concrete excesses of many hospitals and doctors," and he set forth as health tools rotating funds for agricultural projects, small animal and garden programs and development of locally controlled cooperatives. In Haiti he found church-sponsored workers admirably dedicated to "motivating people to reflect on themselves and their situation and to involve themselves in decisions bearing on their own life and death, which are prerequisites to effective action of any kind."

The clinic files include studies conducted by others in highland villages. The doctor pointed ruefully to 62 anthropological investigations performed in San Pedro La Laguna (a village with a beach), whose chief residual was confusion in the minds of the villagers. He responded briskly to certain "needs assessments" by "development professionals" who found in the indigenous peoples a "passivity" requiring motivational training. In his view, the highland peoples were quintessential marketeers and their passivity was best judged in the light of their profound appreciation of nature, their immediate practical response to violent upheavals like the earthquake of 1976 and their survival through 500 years of domination. They remain to this day the actual (though woesomely undercompensated) producers of most Guatemalan products, which are concentrated in agriculture, textiles and crafts.

THE LIGHT ALSO RISES

In 1975 the World Health Organization cited the Chimaltenango program as one of ten models worldwide for effective health promotion. In 1976 this project was featured in the first of a series of documentary films by the Christian Medical Commission of the World Council of Churches entitled *Seeds of Health*. In 1978 this film was shown at a world meeting of health leaders in Kazakhstan and contributed to the substance of the Alma-Ata Declaration and Report on Primary Health Care. All of this helped make Chimaltenango a surprising crossroads for primary health care advocates and for study of survival and development strategies on the part of indigenous peoples.

Ten later papers in this book have been prepared by noted anthropologists, physicians and teachers of physicians, agriculturalists, primary health care exponents and community developers in various parts of the world who intersected with the Chimaltenango program and found their own activities profoundly affected by it. (Their profiles are listed, for ready reference, at the very end of this book.) Six writers were among the hundreds of medical students, Peace Corps Volunteers, World Neighbors staff and work campers who enjoyed tours of dutiful learning with the program. The very diversity of these papers reflects the integrative approach of the Maya to their problems and the breadth of interest to be found in Behrhorst himself. We expect the readers, like the writers, will include North American students and professionals, theologians and parishioners, medics, agricultural extensionists, community organizers, overseas aid specialists and volunteers, Central America watchers and lovers of Guatemala as well as citizens seeking appropriate ways to meet or authentic ways to touch the people of this lavishly colored yet grievously and ceaselessly tortured neighbor country.

All the writers of these more-than-memorial essays draw from this Guatemala project understandings and practices needed in many more places today. They point to the importance of cultural understandings for healing practices and to health and disease as cultural understandings. They show how medical education can lead one to such a place and how that place can alter one's views of education. They look toward more creative combinations of medicine and public health, and toward more cooperative ways by which professional and technical workers can join people in their current struggles with health problems. They reaffirm the authority of communities for organizing health provisions and see health as a primary issue for organizing communities.

The contributors put these principles to work with respect to particular communities in particular places and with respect to special maladies and special strategies. (Also with respect to the multitudes in our world, including Guatemalans, who have lost their places in the world and live to return intact.) A writer from Senegal illustrates a Behrhorst influence, extending both from Chimaltenango and from Tulane, by describing how his society adds modern medicine to its folkways without loss of cohesiveness. A former colleague writes from Ghana where he is helping the people to breed up corn, as did the early Guatemalans. These writers do not all strike the same notes; two, for example, select and interpret international health data very differently. But all choose to speak of healthy communities exercising capacities and not simply about health providers meeting needs.

Our last two essays (before the final word from Chimaltenango) describe a translation of learnings from Chimaltenango to certain communities in hyper-typical modern cities, including the South Bronx in New York and the West Side of Chicago. The Chicago writer met Behrhorst for the first time during the early 1970s when they were correspondents and participants in a series of critical, cross-cultural, historically competent and relentlessly probing inquiries into alternative approaches to health care that were then taking place at Centro Intercultural de Documentación (CIDOC) in Cuernavaca, Morelos, Mexico. In the papers selected for this book Behrhorst continues to use critical terms like "sick life" and constructive terms like "conviviality" which he drew from those discussions (Illich 1973, 1976).

After the inquirers at CIDOC had named "basic determinants of health" and were turning toward constructive models, they found that intellectuals were no longer very useful and neither were most medics, including "progressive" ones. When it came to putting fundamental concepts into actual practice with people, our Chicago essayist recalls, it was Behrhorst who proved the most inventive participant of all. Beginning from the two most fundamental determinants of health—the relationship of people to the earth on which they stand and to the community in which they move—this doctor joined his people in the healthy adventure of "making a new path by walking it." He was a rarity: a humble physician—in the sense that the Mayan people themselves are said to be "humble."

Doctor means "teacher." To this doctor-teacher and the Kaqchikel with whom he went to school, and to some of their previous learners, we now commend the reader. People in the highland villages of Guatemala, Nuevo Amanecer members and workers in Chimaltenango, and both the Guatemalan and the North American foundations are pleased to be able to reach you in this way. They would be very pleased to have you reach back to them. All hope you read these papers in good health.

ACKNOWLEDGMENTS

The Behrhorst foundations, south and north, supported the preparation of these papers with good will, patience and hands-on cooperation. Members of the Guatemalan board and staff made manuscripts and memories available. Dr. James Hogan, president of the board in North America, brought his experience in Guatemala and his medical-ethical judgment to review and interpret sensitive materials from the Chimaltenango program during the violence of the early 1980s. Richard Margoluis worked through reports made by Carroll Behrhorst of visits to medical programs in Asia, Africa, Haiti and New Guinea. Brian Leo Treacy made choices among oft-told stories for use in introducing the story teller. Patricia O'Connor sifted documents of the various programs in the highland villages. John Puelle helped select communications following the earthquake of 1976. O'Connor, Treacy and Puelle also served as early readers. Patricia Krause was a never failing source of information from the foundation and an ingratiating channel to some of its friends.

We are grateful for permission to reprint certain previously published materials. To Ulli Steltzer for reproduction of photographs and expressions of Kaqchikel workers, many of which appeared in her *Health in the Guatemalan Highlands* (Seattle: University of Washington Press, 1983), and for use of Behrhorst's description of the Chimaltenango Development Program as prepared for that volume. A statement by Francisco Currichich, which appears with his picture in a chapter on the violence in the highlands, is from the film *Seeds of Health* (1976), produced by Film Oikumene and Teldok Films. A film summary prepared by director Peter Krieg is cited by Behrhorst in chapter eight.

Some of our writers have drawn from themselves. The introduction by Ralph Crawshaw makes some use of a previous report in his *Club of KOS* newsletter (April, 1986) and of an obituary he wrote for the *Journal of the American Medical Association* 264(October 24/31,1990):16. Jonathan Horton recovers comments from a 25th anniversary report from Chimaltenango which he prepared for the *New England Journal of Medicine* 316(June 25, 1987):1666-1669. Victor Sidel's essay draws from a lecture to the Canadian Public Health Association that was published in the *Canadian Journal of Public Health* 70 (July, 1979): 234-239. John McKnight's story in chapter 19 was previously told in a consultation of the Dag Hammarskjöld Foundation in Uppsala, Sweden, and published in *Development Dialogue* 1978(1).

A PHYSICIAN'S INTRODUCTION

HUMAN BEING AND PHYSICIAN

Ralph Crawshaw

"Kansas Doctor at Work in Guatemala"—this story of the 1960s was unusual enough to gain worldwide attention. In 1975 the World Health Organization cited the Behrhorst Foundation in Guatemala as an exemplary model, worldwide, of effective rural health care. But to fully appreciate the import of these papers from and about the work of Carroll Behrhorst with the peoples of highland Guatemala we will need an eye that sees through popular and professional recognition to the adventure of the man himself. The best lens is one that focuses his lifelong pursuit of a question—one that grew in the highlands to pursue him and those with whom he lived and worked.

The land which produced Behrhorst was not Guatemala but Kansas, USA. Flat, open and stable, this agricultural state had not had any active volcano, earthquake or landslide for eons, nor any tropical diseases. Yet for an attentive Behrhorst growing up in the Kansas of the early 20th century there were already questions.

During the 1930s nature devastated the attempts of Kansas farmers to conquer the prairie. Drought ravaged both land and people. Dust storms, tornados or grasshoppers could wipe out a Kansas town almost as swiftly as an earthquake. During the border wars of the 1860s brother had killed brother over land. During the Great Depression farmers were driven from their fields by finance and machinery, just as surely as family cornfields were turning into plantations in Guatemala. It was a time of landlessness, unemployment, widespread malnutrition, neglected and unchecked diseases, destitute and migrant families. Kansas proved a school with a primary curriculum on the problems humans encounter in facing nature and one another.

Behrhorst came to questions of human health like a bee to blossoms, naturally and relentlessly. After graduating from the Washington University School of Medicine in St. Louis, Missouri, in 1947, he continued training in family medicine at the University of Cincinnati Hospitals, St. Louis City Hospital and St. Joseph's Hospital in Alton, Illinois, and also served as a naval medical officer with the fleet marine forces. He returned to Winfield, Kansas, to establish a family medical practice.

But from the start Behrhorst had looked toward a practice of medicine in a less developed or, as he might say, otherwise developed country. In the late 1950s, he made several trips to Guatemala under the auspices of a religious organization. By 1962 he closed his Kansas practice to move with his family to Guatemala City and Antigua. His formal association with the medical mission came loose when he found his way to the highlands where, to speak only of the Department of Chimal-tenango, there were virtually no functioning medical facilities for a Maya-Kaqchikel population of 140,000.

The issue of the availability of medical services deepened into one concerning the adequacy of such services as existed in addressing the conditions of disease. This became for him a point of basic understanding that bordered on the theological—the very definition of health and its principles. Healing was growing in his view to include maintenance of identity, restoration of dignity and self-respect, and exercise of personal human functions that are more than physiological. Guatemala was the place for him but there had to be a better way. He rented a house in Chimaltenango —then a town of 20,000 which served as a hub for Kaqchikel villages — trained local women as aids, opened a house clinic, cured diseases and nursed his question.

Behrhorst confronted problems of health that would overwhelm any but the strongest physician. On his emerging definition of care — "helping those who need help to help themselves" — he now turned attention to the conditions associated with malnutrition, dehydration, respiratory infections and parasitic diseases, including contaminated water, polluted earth, lack of land and violence. He was determined to assist the people toward managing their problems within their resources.

The clinic in Chimaltenango remained small — two regular physicians and a dozen nurses — yet it flourished as a teaching center for a whole new breed of indigenous health workers. Here young Mayans, selected by their communities, received training in the basics for work in their own villages. Behrhorst staunchly resisted the temptation to appeal for outside help in the form of advanced Western medicines, choosing instead to pursue techniques that would allow local health provisions to grow on their own.

A small hospital of 70 beds grew up with the clinic, also with an objective of raising health understandings and initiatives. Families came along to the hospital to cook for and help with the care of their sick members. The staff used this opportunity to communicate elemental health practices such as dressing wounds, boiling water, digging latrines, and adding vegetables and eggs to their diet.

In addition to these health workers, persons were trained for work with communities in extending and diversifying agriculture, conducting women's programs in nutrition and family health, planning and developing water projects, and conducting a land-loan program — measures that enabled increasing numbers of indigenous Guatemalans to reclaim health in terms of active relations with the land and their community. Unconsciously, Behrhorst used this small site as a point of leverage to move the world.

JOLTING ROUNDS AND ROADS

I visited Chimaltenango in 1985. The clinic is just off the central square, not far from the church, readily accessible. Once through its grated passageway, you enter a grassy courtyard with meeting rooms, labs and wards set back under a tile-covered walkway — a cloister protecting waiting patients from the sun and unpredictable cloudbursts.

To make rounds with "Doc" Behrhorst was to learn from a complete physician. We followed through the sun to a ward where a three-month-old took his full attention. He commented to us without looking up from the child, "Pneumonia in the dehydrated is not easy to treat, but I think this child will pull through." As I looked about at what seemed slim pickings of equipment, he mentioned that the people present were family, including a grandmother who had come along to strengthen the mother who hovered over the baby. This was their way of health and it was now his. His characteristic phrase: "We will have a great deal to talk about tomorrow."

Behrhorst had that direct quality of palaver which characterizes many midwesterners seeking more from voiced mutuality than bare information. He addressed you forthrightly, right to the soul. He moved with the drive of a Kansas wheat farmer bringing in the harvest before a storm. Viking blue eyes, sun-bleached, straw-blonde hair and a healthy corpulence.

The next day we made for the country in a bruised four-door truck with its shocks set for a ten-ton load. Behrhorst wished to talk with an indigenous health worker, one of his team of "health promoters." We quickly ran out of paved highway and, while bouncing along, he regaled us with facts: no hypertensive cardio-vascular diseases, hernias, varicose veins or rectal carcinomas were to be found here. In contrast, continuous wood smoke from cooking, along with changes in climate when men go to work on coffee plantations along the coast, caused serious respiratory diseases. Hunger, contaminated water and accumulated wastes produced stomach disorders. Gifts of medicine from the states often matched needs of the givers rather than those of the sick in Guatemala.

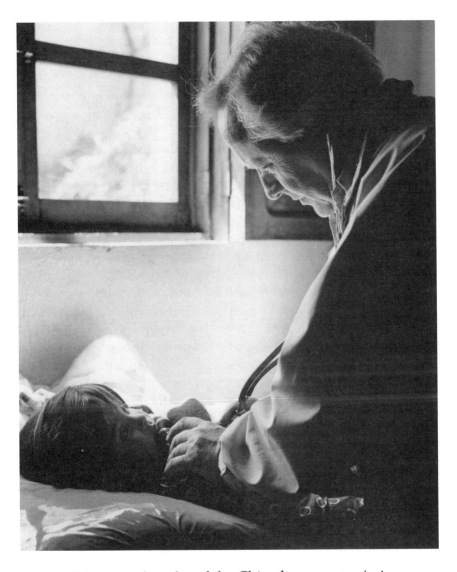

Carroll Behrhorst, founder of the Chimaltenango project, examining a child. "This child needs land."

We wound down dirt roads, cut into the sides of ravines, crossing the streams at the bottom. Here blossoms of women and children were washing rainbow-hued skirts and blouses on water-covered rocks and drying them, sun-strewn on the grass, with a sociality which for sheer, exulting human spirit might shame a cathedral of true believers. Once by them, it was up the cut in the far side of the ravine to the next plateau.

The region was comparatively safe at this time, although it had not been so just a few years back. To make the point, Behrhorst explained that a village of sixty-seven families we were now passing through included sixty-seven widows since a day in 1982 when all the men were lined up and shot. Not satisfied with the slaughter, the armed visitors also burned the crops on the hillside. The following year other combatants turned up to burn new crops which the widows had planted. There was no question that these people knew the sharpest meaning of human hunger.

The man we wished to visit was one of the few surviving members of an original team of health promoters. Suddenly, there he was, a dust-covered, sweating farmer struggling down a mountain path with a bag of compost on his shoulder. Out jumped Behrhorst. The man dropped his burden. Together they hugged and shouted their joy.

The promoter's surgery was a concrete block building with steps leading up to a porch over a weathered wooden door. Inside, out of the sun, we sat in a circle on upright painted chairs. Sacks of corn concealed one wall, while a curtain partially screened off the other end where stood a chipped white table and battered metal trays holding simple instruments. On the front wall hung a poster encouraging hand washing and a certificate from the Behrhorst clinic. The view framed by the door of a distant smoking volcano over a verdant valley seemed even more awesome from our humble surrounding.

We listened to this promoter's recent success in suturing a nasty scalp wound with needle and thread, his pleasure at convincing every farmer in the neighborhood to build a latrine and his anticipation of community plans to draw clean water from a mountain source using not mechanical pumps but gravity — which would require advice but not a visit from a gringo engineer. His wife interrupted by setting before us a jug of hot coffee and a plate of fresh-baked bread wrapped in a large blue napkin with embroidered red and green flowers. With this sacrament of hospitality the talk moved closer to the bone. This promoter attributed the survival of his town to a solidarity in isolating itself as much as possible from both warring sides.

DIFFICULT QUESTIONS

Violence, proved to be one of Behrhorst's most daunting problems. Guatemala has been, and remains, a land of violent political turmoil. For years government troops and armed guerrillas have struggled for control of the countryside. In accordance with one of the oldest traditions of the medical profession, Behrhorst remained officially neutral in the political struggle. The political beliefs of the wounded went unstated while casualties from both sides were treated in the hospital.

Such neutrality did not exempt Behrhorst or his staff from threats of death. In 1983 a combatant gunned down one of the doctors near the hospital grounds. At the end of the year only eighteen of forty-five trained health promoters in the Department of Chimaltenango were alive and accounted for. When all international agencies recalled their medical teams from Guatemala, the Behrhorst clinic and hospital carried on. Each afternoon the doctor walked the entire length of the town to let everyone know the clinic staff was not intimidated and would carry on its proper work despite the dangers.

Nor did such neutrality leave Behrhorst a moral bystander. He was part of the clinic, the clinic part of the town, the district, the country of suffering people. In training health promoters he was raising their visibility and their vulnerability to violence. Each death or disappearance of a health promoter brought an anguished sense of complicity in spite of good intentions.

Behrhorst cooperated with other programs. He spoke of his work with *Agrosalud*, a minimal health maintenance organization for 18,000 plantation workers. He made arrangements for me to meet with some of the health workers when they flew in for their

Training health promoters in the campo near Chimaltenango.

monthly meeting in Zone 1, a less-than-fancy part of Guatemala City. I found the place, a small office with the now-typical heavy door and guard, and sat among stacks of simple medical supplies to listen. Behrhorst had prepared me for the meeting with a comment that framed the entire enterprise, "Remember, it takes two fingers to pick one coffee bean, so each morning your coffee is brought to you on the basis of an economy of poverty."

Here were four health workers who practiced in an area where less than one-half of one percent of the population had health services. The owners of the coffee plantations now contributed five cents per month per worker for a health system which trained indigenous people as primary health care workers to treat diseases of plantation employees, while also educating them in sanitation, nutrition and self-help. For the seriously ill the system was backed up with a referral service to such places as the Behrhorst clinic. Two key points of the program were inclusion of owners on local health boards and provision of five acres of land on which workers could farm for themselves after 4:00 p.m., quitting time on a plantation.

The men asked questions about my country and were amazed to hear that we too have many millions without access to formal health care, that we have disease-causing technology, single-parent communities, and neglect of preventive and prenatal practices for the sake of high technology. This led to consideration of different modes of allocating health resources, a worldwide problem, and once again raised questions of life and death.

THE QUESTION TO US ALL

Looking back on the quality of Behrhorst's "health care" brings to mind an old Russian proverb: "A doctor always leaves a bit of his heart with the patient." The amount of heart this doctor left in Guatemala turned out to be considerably more than a bit. To some it seems that he gave his whole heart—but that is not so, for he was a wise man, not a saint, and he knew that love in obvious large doses can be damaging. He knew that heart sharing, especially by people who were not natives, had its acknowledged limits.

Though he took the Kaqchikels of Guatemala's highlands to heart, he sought to sustain rather than burden them with his caring. They remained who they were, stronger not weaker for his ministrations. Both gained, neither lost. Both grew in knowledge, power, self-respect, and personal autonomy. Both recognized and shared the natural human fate.

As you read these papers in a library, at your desk, in a summer swing, or perhaps between emergency calls, imagine yourself in Guatemala. Place yourself down at the end of a hospital courtyard in Chimaltenango. Come onto the portico out of the bright sun. Look up at the magnificent view of a smoking volcano, the burning blue sky with its many-staired silvery-grey clouds percolating to great heights in preparing a thundering evening bombardment on all below. See the old Kaqchikel man in the carrying chair at the other end of the courtyard smiling at his two grandchildren. Sit here on the long, hard pine bench and brace your back against the spalled, earthquake-cracked wall behind you.

Then remember, as you read these papers, the afternoon walk of this doctor. While he often invited us to visit Guatemala for its beauty, he never asked us to put our feet exactly in his footsteps. What he asked was that we all join people somewhere on a road to health. The first responsibility of any physician or other professional worker is to be a complete human being among humans, even if it means each day walking some dangerous village square of one's own.

I know of some—there must be many physicians among the 400,000 who practice in the United States—with courage to take this common road, though at present our profession appears to lack a larger language for speaking of that. This is the caring that physicians share with humanity, the rest is technicality. When we openly address the challenge of personal and social completeness, physician to patient, physician to community, physician to nature, day in day out, our profession will overflow with vitality and a blossoming of Behrhorst centers, worldwide, will become inevitable.

The hospital at Chimaltenango.

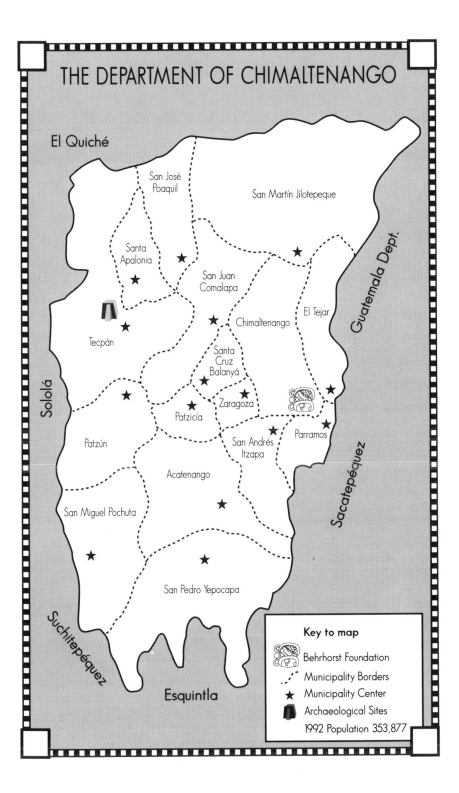

THE DEPARTMENT OF CHIMALTENANGO

El Quiché

San José Poaquil

San Martín Jilotepeque

Santa Apalonia

San Juan Comalapa

El Tejar

Guatemala Dept.

Tecpán

Chimaltenango

Santa Cruz Balanyá

Sololá

Zaragoza

Patzicía

Parramos

Patzún

San Andrés Itzapa

Sacatepéquez

Acatenango

San Miguel Pochuta

San Pedro Yepocapa

Suchitepéquez

Esquintla

Key to map

Behrhorst Foundation

Municipality Borders

★ Municipality Center

Archaeological Sites

1992 Population 353,877

Department of Chimaltenango
Behrhorst Foundation, Collaborating Villages by Municipality

Acatenango
Pacoc
Pajales
Quisaché
San Antonio Nejapa
San José Tziquinyá

Chimaltenango
Bola de Oro
Ciénaga Grande
San Jacinto
San Marcos Pacoc
Santa Isabel
Santa María de Jesús
Triunfo de la Juventud

El Tejar
Santo Domingo

Parramos

Patzicía
Cerro Alto
La Esperanza
Patzicía

Patzún
Chipiacul
Las Mercedes
San Lorenzo Cojobal

San Andrés Itzapa
Chimachoy
San José Calderas

San José Poaquil
Chiraxaj
Pacul
Poaquil

San Juan Comalapa
Chimazat
Comalapa
Pamumus
Panabajal

Patzaj
San Juan Comalapa
Simajuleu
Xenimajuyú

San Martín Jilotepeque
Chi don Juan
Chijocom
Chuabaj Grande
Chuabajito
Chuatalum
Cojumachaj
El Oratorio
El Rosario Canajal
Las Escobas
Quimal
San Antonio Cornejo
Tioxya
Xejuyú

San Miguel Pochuta

San Pedro Yepocapa
Santa Sofía
Yucales

Santa Apalonia
Chiquex
Chucacay
La Vega
Pacután
Palay
Parajbey
Patzaj
Xeabaj
Xecoil

Santa Cruz Balanyá

Tecpán
Aguas Escondidas
Caquixajay
Chichoy
Chiquinjuyú, Xenimajuyú

El Tesoro
Los Potrerillos
Pachaj
Pacorral, Panabajal
Pacután, Panabajal
Pamesul
San José Chirijuyu
Tecpán
Xejabi
Xepac
Xetonox, Panabajal
Xocobil, Panabajal

Zaragoza
Rincón Chiquito
Rincón Grande

Other Departments in Guatemala

El Quiché
Macalajao
San Miguel Uspantán
Xola

Esquintla
San Andrés Osuma

Sacatepéquez
El Rejón
San Miguel Dueñas
Sumpango

Sololá
Chirij Cruz
Churaxón
El Encanto
Los Ciprales
Paximbal
San Andrés Semetabaj
Xajaxac

Suchitepéquez
Matzatenango

VOICES OF THE KAQCHIKEL

I am renting three cuerdas (3 X 39 yards square) that I use here to grow wheat and corn. I pay my rent by cultivating two cuerdas for the landlord in Panunul, which is ten kilometers for me to walk each way. Nothing makes ends meet. I can go neither forward nor back. I lack many things, but the origin of my problem is lack of land. I can't seem to find a way to change my situation. In previous years I went to the coast to work, but you don't earn much there and there is sickness: headaches, stomachaches, pain in your lungs. Of the three little houses, only the straw on the roofs is mine.

— Inocente Otzoy Colaj, tenant farmer in Simajuleu
(Steltzer, 1983)

I have always worked in the fields, planting corn, beans, and wheat. This is my real work. A committee selected me to study with the Behrhorst program to be a promoter. Now the people ask me about things they want to know—for example, plant diseases. We have also got better sheep through the program and now have finer wool. It is my job to orient people toward new ideas and to do agricultural experiments. Now only one percent of the people in this community need to go to work at the coast.

> — *Baltazar Yat Chipel, health promoter in Xola, Quiché*
> *(Steltzer, 1983)*

I have lived the problems in the villages... Nobody advised me how to do this job. Observing the manner in which the doctor worked, I decided to walk in the same path. It is easy to talk about health but difficult to practice. One often finds oneself placed between a wall and a sword. Curing diseases without touching their origins is an error. A sick and malnourished person might recover here at the hospital but, confronted with the same situation at home, will soon get sick again... I ask the promoters to get the patient's history, listen to the symptoms and prescribe the appropriate treatment [but] the most important thing is the prevention of diseases.... Meeting with each other we become aware. Working together we have strength.

> — *Carlos Xoquic, health promoter, coordinator of promoters,*
> *now president of the Fundación in Chimaltenango*
> *(Steltzer, 1983)*

1

WHAT DID WE HAVE TO TEACH THE DOCTOR?

María Hortensia Otzoy de Cap
Interview and translation by John Puelle

When Carroll Behrhorst came to Guatemala he learned from us how to respect the Mayan culture. He learned how to appreciate our language and dialects, our food, our customs, our ways and our religion. He learned this on visits to the homes of people in San Jacinto and La Bola de Oro, which we made along with him. He would enter the houses and sit and talk with the people. He also learned much on visits to the homes of the health promoters in villages such as San José Poaquil, Patzún and Chipiacul.

First, he had to learn the customs of arriving in a home, where the people would give him something. They would give the doctor not coffee but beer, and he had to drink it. They gave him beer because for them it was a great joy when the doctor arrived. I told him that the people were making a gift of the beer, so he had to drink it. Or they gave him a cup of *kuxa* (a homemade

Hortensia Otzoy de Cap recruiting women in the market
of San Martín Jelotepeque.

hard liquor) and he had to drink it because we were there on a visit. We went with him and he learned.

One of the things the doctor learned well was the physical type of each Mayan person and the characteristics that were typical of each town. He came to recognize that a person was from Sumpango just by looking at him or her. He also learned to recognize the face types of people from San José Poaquil, Comalapa, Tecpán and other places, differentiating the faces of people according to their villages. He did this so that he would know about a person's history, habits and conditions and whether a person needed special help—whether, for example, a person wanted medicine but couldn't pay for it. If the doctor did not know a person's name, he would describe that person by the face type. "He has the face of someone from Poaquil," he would say.

The doctor learned how the people live in their homes. He paid close attention to the work of the women, like weaving, by going to their houses and watching them. He asked and listened and learned. He learned how the people live together with their animals, their chickens, dogs and pig.

It was not easy to separate the people from all this when they needed to go to the hospital and get treatment. That is why the doctor said that they could all come and stay in the hospital. If they have chickens, he said, they should bring them and put them under the bed. If they have dogs, they should bring them along and take care of them at the hospital. He learned that people have to have their tortillas, so he made a kitchen at the hospital. "Let them make their tortillas here," he said. When he had learned about weaving, he said, "Let them bring their loom and their work, they can weave here." The construction of the hospital was itself a result of his learning our culture. The hospital and clinic were like the old houses before the earthquake with a covered porch for sitting and talking.

The doctor learned everything when we went on visits to the towns where he wanted to start development work—towns where we first practiced medicine so that now we can work there. He learned from the customs and the culture, and he always asked me whether something he was going to do or say was good or bad in the eyes of the people. "Is this OK?" he would ask. And I'd say that it was. He learned a few Kaqchikel words, only a few, but enough to ask the people in Kaqchikel whether their stomach hurt or where they were hurting.

He learned about the food, the vegetables, the leaves, the herbs and the seeds. He would say to me, "We have to teach nutrition on the basis of what is already being eaten in the community." He would ask me, "How do you prepare this herb, this tea, this fruit, this seed, this vegetable?" I taught him about the good plants and herbs, like *quelite* (greens), *chipilín* (a mimosa species) and *bledo* (a spinach). I taught him and he said, "Tell the people the good things. Tell them to eat the things that you say are good." But he never learned to eat *güicoy* (a zucchini-like squash) — he didn't like it.

The doctor learned here in Guatemala to carry his billfold around his waist. If a woman said that she had no husband or money to pay the bill or to buy food, the doctor would ask me if this was true. Then he would take out his billfold and would give her money. He would give money to the widows and the needy people so they could buy their food. He did not do this at the beginning, only after he came to know Chimaltenango.

The doctor understood that one should never hurt the feelings of the people. He learned that the Mayan people are sincere and very humble. He also learned that we have dignity and pride. He learned this from our language and our religion, and from our clothing that is woven with meanings, like a book that can be worn, and is different in each town.

These, then, are some of the things that the doctor learned from me and from my people.

Home production in Comalapa.

Suppertime.

2

A CONVERSATION ON MAYA-KAQCHIKEL CONCEPTS AND PRACTICES OF HEALTH

Juanita Batzibal Tujal
With Mario Noj, Antonio Martínez, and Richard Luecke

What do Mayan peoples mean by "health" and "healing"? How does this compare with ideas and practices in Western industrial societies?

Our ideas of health are in many ways similar to those of other people. Health, as understood by the Maya, is a state of "equilibrium" and sickness is a condition of "disequilibrium" — whether among the parts of an organism or with the larger community and environment. Healing means that something is done to help restore the natural balance.

Mayan treatment differs most obviously from that of modern Western societies in that our elder-physicians are themselves members of the community they serve. They are always available when we need them — I think this is not the case with Western doctors. I remember occasions on which members of my family experienced severe disorders late at night. For example, my father once suffered severe stomach pains with diarrhea and vomiting at a late hour and we were afraid that he might die. But the Western doctor did not wish to get out of bed. A local woman healer came quickly and calmed the disease by using *manzanilla* (*oliva sp*) and *pericón* (*Tagetes lucida*). Similarly, our midwives are never far away and they come at any hour of the day or night. Thus, our healers are recognized and loved for being with us when we need them.

Moreover, the person in a state of disequilibrium is always treated as part of a family and a community. What this person needs, as a matter of first importance, is to receive attention, reassurance and support by the larger community. The community is like a larger body—in fact *is* a larger body—and when one member is malfunctioning that affects us all. Ours is a social vision of health and this is never lost sight of along the way.

Our healers are "elders," so-called not because they are old but because they use a practiced wisdom which began with our forebears. They are sometimes called *curanderos*, which unfortunately might suggest to some people something like "witch doctors." They are, rather, wise men and wise women who know the Mayan traditions concerning health and healing and who have themselves closely observed community members and the effects that plants and herbs have on their patients. They are, in this sense, scientists. Their observations and practices proceed from, and add to, those that have been used for many centuries with their own people.

What is the relation of health to the land? To work? To God?

The Maya see themselves as a part of nature. There is no way that we can see ourselves as outside of nature or as struggling against nature. Rather, we see health as functioning within nature on the basis of natural relationships. When our people go down to the coast to work on plantations their health often declines because their bodies know and are accommodated to our Guatemalan highland. Elsewhere we are out of context and this can have physical, mental and spiritual effects. That is why our people feel tied to their land, why they respect the land and care for it—because we both give sense to the land and receive sense from the land. Disrupting this relationship causes disequilibrium. Restoring it is healing.

Work for us is considered sacred because work just *is* our relationship with the land and because work builds up the community. So we are grateful for land, for work, for community and for health all at the same time. We are grateful to *el corazón del cielo* (which is both "the heart of the sky" and "the heart of the earth") that there should be this connection among all these things. We think of land and work as gifts and of "the heart of the earth" as giver and healer. But we do not think of illness as a punishment.

Will you describe treatments that take place in times of sickness and say something about the ceremonies that attach to healing?

Usually people know when they are in a state of disequilibrium. Mothers know this about their children through constant observation of them. Our wise men and women—our scientists and healers—know when disequlibrium is the case for the same reason, not by the use of technical instruments or measurements but by close observation of actions and attitudes and by asking careful questions. Our healers make much use of dialogue on the way to deciding with someone what is to be done.

We use balancing terms, "hot" and "cold," to refer to causes of disequilibrium and the necessary cures. When a person goes to the coast and suffers a chest paralysis we say "the 'cold' took him or her." This may at first sound contradictory since it is hot on the coast, but the treatment needed to restore equilibrium to that person is actually something warm. Our "hot" and "cold" herbs and teas have been used for generations to restore balance.

Because they are natural and reinstate a natural balance, these plants and herbs are viewed as sacred. Similarly, our sacred places are natural places, not temples but mountains and volcanos. Our ceremonies always take place around a fire.

That is the meaning of our health-related ceremonies. We have ceremonies asking for health, ceremonies for purifying herbs and ceremonies to attend the sick. The purpose is always to affirm, strengthen and celebrate our relationship to the earth and our relationship to one another in the Mayan community.

What is the role of the healers? How does one get to be a healer?

Our healers are elders in the sense of being wise men and women whose wisdom has come from our forebears and is used for the good of our community. We do use physical terms to describe and locate pain—we say we have a "stomach ache" or a "head ache." But healing also depends on confidence that the prescribed ministrations are in accordance with nature and with the long experience of the community. Thus, our healing is physical, psychological, social and spiritual. It includes "mind over body."

Our elder-healers are not trained in universities and are not trained today from books. We know there were formerly great books of Mayan science: mathematics, astronomy, history, psychology, religion and medicine. But these were burned after the conquest. As a result, we rely on oral traditions for the use of herbs and other practices that have survived the test of time. Our more experienced elders prepare new Mayan healers by passing on such received knowledge and the new elders then become accepted by the community. Their method includes continuing close observation of the functions and the mutual effects of plants and animals, of our own interrelation with these, and careful memory of fresh experiments and their results.

That is how we came to know, for example, that *camomila* tea (*matricaria camomilla*) is good for stress and high blood pressure; that *pericón* (*Tagetes lucida*) quiets stomach ache and loosens constipation; that a tea combining marigold, orange leaves and *hierbabuena* (*menthe sp*) stops diarrhea. Generations have known, and our own experience confirms, that the discomfort of a cold can be relieved by a tea combining coffee, lemon, ginger, cloves, black

Fruits of the field near Macalajao, Quiché.

pepper and cinnamon, and that an ordinary cough can be soothed with a cooked combination of ginger, toasted tangerine peel, eucalyptus, chocolate and drops of lemon, or with a single herb that we call *gordolobo* (*verbascum thapsus* or *graphalium sp*). Eucalyptus leaves in boiled water will reduce a fever or, when breathed, will calm a cough. Garlic juice will counter parasites. A pine sap mixed with *sábila* (*aloe vera*) and black soap, melted over fire, moderates the pain and speeds the healing of a burn or sore. When the cord is cut after childbirth, we cover the wound with powdered tobacco and wrap it with fresh tobacco leaves to protect it and ensure healing. There are plants that boost energy and flowers that strengthen the immune system. Drug manufacturers are analyzing the plants that we use to find the active agents in them.

We do not ourselves use chemical medicines because they are less accessible to us. They are also patented and controlled by people outside the community and cannot be studied by us in terms of their long-term effects. Sometimes, when we are required to take the medicines of "outside" doctors, we find that these do give some relief but do not really heal. They make us feel better, but in some cases also create problems in other parts of the body or at a later time.

How does this view of health affect marriage, child bearing, family planning, etc.?

Marriage is natural and basic for life. Husbands and wives are like members of one body. Sex is a normal physical and social necessity — it is not "sin." If a man or woman is forced to remain alone, without a partner, madness may result.

It is difficult for us to accept "family planning" in the sense of changing something in the natural processes of the body, either those of the mother or those of the child to be. For the same reason, it is difficult for us to think of changing one's organs or changing one's sex. We do practice a form of family planning, and are talking about this among ourselves, but such planning is done without altering the body and is conducted in consultation with

3

GRINGO DOCTOR—THE LEGEND
AND THE LEGACY

Felipa Xico Ajquejay
Read in the Chimaltenango Square at the death of the doctor
Translation by the editor

Carroll Behrhorst was not only a professional and competent man but also a friend and companion who chose to place himself on the road of history with the dispossessed of the Department of Chimaltenango, Guatemala. He did this specifically with the Kaqchikel, a proud and dignified people who love life and work but are impoverished by the condition they have inherited from the Spanish conquest. We therefore invite all our friends to join us in invoking God on our remembrances and grief at this time, so that the doctor's wisdom may fall like the seed of a sower on fertile ground and the harvest may be in accordance with his high purpose. That purpose was the self-determination of our peoples and villages. In order for this to come to pass, it is important for us to think back over the life and work of the doctor among us.

At the outset of the 1960s Doctor Behrhorst faced a decision between two possibilities for offering his life and his capacities, one in India and the other in Guatemala. God illumined him to decide for Guatemala and, through auspices of the Lutheran church, he came to our country.

In 1962 he made his first extended visits through Chimaltenango, spending much of his time in the village of San Jacinto. After seeing and reflecting on the needs of this area, he decided to establish a clinic in the departmental hub of Chimaltenango. Here he saw the same sick people coming back again and again with the same diseases in spite of whatever treatments they may have received. He knew these problems of sickness and health would never be overcome unless the people instituted some basic changes.

Previously the doctor had looked at illness in such a way as to say, "By curing patients we will overcome disease." Now he faced the fact that this was a misleading idea, since people were coming back with the same infirmities produced by the same causes. He now said that curing the sick in clinics and hospitals was "like trying to empty the Atlantic Ocean with a teaspoon." This might serve to make the professional staff feel busy and useful and it might cause the whole world to marvel at their dedication—but they would be marvelling at nothing more than a teaspoon.

The doctor recognized, of course, that a facility would be needed in some cases, alongside more basic programs for disease prevention and health promotion. Accordingly, he created the *hospitalito* and trained a staff from the region who spoke the Kaqchikel dialect and belonged to the indigenous culture. Some of these were to work in the hospital and others were to serve as links with the communities.

THE EXTENSION OF HEALTH WORK

In 1966 we saw the beginning both of training health promoters and of conducting agricultural extension services. At the same time, assessment centers were introduced in several communities — Bola de Oro, Ciénaga Grande, San Jacinto, Cerro Alto and Santa

Family cooking at the Chimaltenango Hospital.

Foot bathing, washing, and questioning piped and tapped water at the pila of the hospital.

Isabel—which would enable us to offer assistance that accorded with the felt needs and expressed will of the people. During the same year, a day clinic was established at San Andrés Osuna in the Department of Escuintla with the purpose of preparing health promoters for that region.

By 1969 day clinics had been opened in Chipiacul, in the community on the former large estate "Las Mercedes" near Patzún, and in Xajaxac of Sololá. Agricultural extension programs, along with programs of health education and nutrition, were in the planning stages with San Martín Jilotepeque and Tecpán.

During the decade of the 1970s the doctor initiated and developed many activities and programs, including the following.

- Purchase and distribution of land through an organization subsequently called "ULEU Foundation" (Kaqchikel for "land"). This organization has achieved independence.

- Establishment of further work in agricultural extension.

- Education of administrative and technical personnel who would put into practice the principles of integral community development that the doctor carried in his mind and heart.

- Extension work with women for nutrition, disease prevention and home education.

- Formation of a sanitation program for acquiring potable water and treating waste in villages of the Chimaltenango area.

- Promotion and organization of a savings and credit association, called Katokí Quetzal Cooperative, through efforts by some of the staff and promoters.

- Promotion and organization of an association of community health programs.

- Cooperation in the formation of the Christian Council of Development Agencies and the Kaqchikel Coordinating Council for Integral Development.

- After the earthquake of 1976, coordination of emergency medical assistance with the central health board and active participation in the reconstruction of housing that had been destroyed.

- Establishment of a program of education for patients with the purpose of cultivating their personal participation in the various aspects of preventive health care.

- Opening of a program of health and agricultural extension in San Miguel Uspantán in the Department of Quiché.

During the early 1980s, it was decided to participate with other non-governmental organizations in an association later called ASINDES (Asociación de Entitades de Desarrollo y Servicios de Guatemala). Also important was the doctor's participation as counselor in the organization Agrosalud, which sought to bring health practices and reform of conditions to plantations.

THE LARGER INFLUENCE OF HIS WORK

The work of the doctor broke new ground not only here but elsewhere.

- He was a precursor in the formation of health promoters and agricultural extensionists as appropriate and necessary collaborators in rural communities. Such training has been widely disseminated at both national and international levels through the testimony of those who benefited and through the doctor's writings.

- In financial matters the doctor maintained and demonstrated responsibility to the leaders of the communities rather than to the more fleeting judgement of donors or outside collaborators.

- He developed capacities for relationship and communication both within communities and with outside authorities and institutions.

- While working in the foundation that bears his name, the doctor demonstrated to all a combination of spirituality, humility, trust and great professional competence, often attending to as many as 200 patients a day in the clinic and the hospital.

Early cooperative farming at Triunfo de la Juventud.

- As part of his efforts to inform and raise fundamental health consciousness in the people of North America and some countries of Europe, the doctor encouraged and facilitated visits by students and multi-disciplinary workers to Chimaltenango. People of many nations have become acquainted with this development program as well as with the fundamental considerations and rationale that underlie its methods.

HIS PHILOSOPHY AND WAY OF WORKING[1]

What we wish most to remember are the principles and the style of the doctor's work.

- In caring for his patients the doctor gave special attention to children. He practiced in accordance with the principle that every single child has the right to a life of dignity as a human being and as an important member of society, present and future.

- In attending his patients he was interested in their problems of sickness and health, not in their money. In the case of patients who did not have money, he would pay for their treatment and meals out of his own pocket.

- In all his work he took cultural values as basic, both respecting them and promoting them. In 1973 he said, "*To be disrespectful in this is a sin.*"

- He spoke out in defense of the dignity and modesty of the indigenous people.

OUR COMMITMENT

Remembering all this, we members of the Nuevo Amanecer organization are fully determined to carry forward the goals and objectives of the Behrhorst program. We will continue to give our

---

[1]Felipa's phrase is *mística de trabajo*. In the previous section we translated *mística* as "spirituality." Here, and in chapter 20 by Carlos Xoquic, we translate the phrase as "way of working." The meanings should be combined.

energies to all the major problems—which in the experience and the judgement of our people are these:

1. Social and economic justice
2. Agricultural production and marketing
3. Production and marketing of crafts
4. Family planning
5. Nutrition
6. Sanitation (water and waste)
7. Curative medicine

The Nuevo Amanecer members find their roots and their vision in a firm belief that "development" is a long-term process, during the course of which people come to speak with "one voice" about their future. The doctor was aware that only a patient process of development will allow us to reach our objectives, and that is why he collaborated in the creation of continuing organizations.

It is essential for us to remember and always to bear in mind that the Behrhorst program is dedicated to the people of this region. It is nevertheless the case that by 1980 many national and international institutions, including the World Health Organization, came to consider our activities a model for community health. As evidence of this wider acceptance, certain programs of the present national government are currently taking our work as a model. If we care to take note, the Ministry of Public Health and Social Assistance are talking about health promoters copied from the Behrhorst program. We also hear the Ministry of Urban and Rural Development proposing a program of promoters for the development of local organizations.

Meanwhile Nuevo Amanecer—the last organization created by the doctor—remains fully aware that the causes and roots of deprivation and underdevelopment have not changed. The basic problems in 1990 are the same as they were in 1960, 1970 and 1980. The list is still the same: low agricultural production, poor nutrition, lack of clean water and sanitation, economic, social and political injustice—above all, lack of participation by the people in managing approaches to health and development problems, which is why many previous strategies have not proved adequate to solve the problems.

SUMMARY

Dr. Behrhorst is accepted and beloved by the poor and dispossessed of Chimaltenango because he was willing to learn from us.

- He learned how to be a friend, especially of the indigenous people.

- Loving life and worthwhile work, he learned that it is necessary to give one's self and to immerse one's self. (He himself considered that he received much more than he gave.)

- Though he was an accomplished and educated man, he learned to live on a level with others, even with the poor, and he thereby acquired the experience necessary to reach the many rural peoples.

- He learned that indigenous people speak from great cultural riches of their own and that humble people have their own profound experiences and understandings.

- He learned that to work with the people is to adapt one's self to local resources. He demonstrated this in his own life and manners, for he did not live in modern style or with modern assumptions.

- He learned to live with the people and share with them. He learned to love the poor and respect the humble, knowing that these very people are capable of resolving their own problems if given the opportunity.

We will not forget.

FROM THE HIGHLANDS
SELECTED PAPERS OF
CARROLL BEHRHORST

Work, if any, would have to be done on their terms and in a manner they understood and could accept. This situation proved educational for me and was a major influence in my personal transformation. What I had learned in my medical training was only partially helpful in healing. The human factors in health and healing were brought home to me. The missioner was being missionized.

— Carroll Behrhorst,
The Chimaltenango Development Program
(1982 Draft)

If dignity, respect, responsibility, honesty, love of life, concern for all things living and hard work are to be used as criteria for humanness, then the Maya rank high on the human scale and have a message for humans everywhere. They understand and love themselves, know and care for one another, and have a natural sense and feeling for the web of life that binds the earth, humans and God together. Though these qualities are socially acquired, they seem almost natural and often appear to exist as do the digestion of food, the rising of the sun and the flowering of the bud.

— Proposal for a youth study center in La Bola de Oro
(1971)

The orientation of our program is not to think in terms of medicines or in terms of disease but rather in terms of health and life, vital life, life together, what Ivan Illich calls "conviviality." Curing is not the important thing. It is much more important to encourage life; and this is not very difficult in Guatemala because the Maya themselves are dedicated to life. They are a very biophilic race. They seem less oppressed by thoughts of pain and death because these, like pain and birth, are considered natural.

— The Chimaltenango Development Program
in Environmental Child Health (1974)

4

"FIRST, A LITTLE STORY FROM CHIMALTENANGO..."

Carroll Behrhorst

MARÍA XICAY OF HER PEOPLE   1962

María, age nine, shy, friendly, intelligent, with copper-brown skin, a warm, round, friendly face and searching black eyes, lives high in the *cordillera*, the mountain spine that separates two oceans to make Central America. Her village is in the Department of Chimaltenango, Guatemala, the northernmost country in Central America. Though it stands in the tropical region of the hemisphere and includes steaming hot coastlands, Guatemala is a "land of eternal spring" with blue-green mountains and fertile valleys, ever-blooming roses, ancient volcanoes, sparkling lakes and bristling pine forests. It is the home of the Maya, descendants of one of the great races and civilizations of all time.

It was here that María's people flowered, creating arts, a hieroglyphic writing system, mathematics, astronomy and a

43

calendar covering vast expanses of time in ways that remain meticulously accurate and awesomely inspiring to the present day. María has inherited a reverence for the human personality, the community and the earth, which has been tended as a sacred fire since the dawn of her race. Her people have concentrated, and in María still concentrate, on the attainment through social ministrations of an adequate human personality that bears responsibility for the web that binds together the earth, community and God.

María and her people are proud, thrifty, honest, hard working, moral and playful. Love of children, respect for the elderly and care of the earth are sacred trusts — in their view, there should be no erosion of the soil or unused waste, no neglect of children, orphans or the aged. Centuries-old habits, herbal cures and sacred rites contribute to a finely balanced adjustment that is also able to absorb some admirable and useful elements from other cultures.

Yet in María's village today disease and poor nutrition take the lives of four out of ten children before they reach the age of five years, as they have for many decades. The death rate of children in rural Guatemala is as high as that of any country on any continent. Moreover, María's story, her way of life and her problems now implicate us, whether we wish to admit it or not. Symbolic of María's nearness to the United States is the fact that every afternoon at two she looks up to see, swiftly passing overhead, a silvery blue and white jet which left the runway at Moisant Airport in New Orleans just two hours before and within minutes will set down in the Valley of the Cows at Guatemala City.

As often as we see María there is something to ponder. The question is whether we can go to work beside her in such a way that, when she grows to womanhood and marries, she need not by reason of disease and poverty return four of ten children to the earth as did her mother. Can she continue her communal way of life with its age-old and self-renewing traditions, even as our culture presses in both with destabilizing influences and with special competencies?

Girl in a field at Macalajao.

LUISA TECÚN CAY AND THE SPIRAL OF DISEASE   1970

Luisa is twenty-eight. She and six children live with a husband who likes work but is landless and often unemployed. Since her marriage ten years ago her lot has been poverty, subsistence home-making and regular pregnancies in a skinny frame. Three years ago she began to cough, which included blood-spitting and caused additional weight loss. She came to the Chimaltenango clinic and the suspected diagnosis was confirmed—advanced tuberculosis.

Luisa felt better with the shots and pills. Ironically, it was then that the real problem began, for after six months she felt well enough, against the counsel of clinic staff, to discontinue her visits for treatment. (The usual treatment extends for eighteen months.) She functioned well for a time, then the cough and blood-spitting recurred. Tests showed reactivation of the infection.

Why did she discontinue her treatment? The answers made sense to her: she felt better, her many chores about the house made it difficult for her to get away, her home was far removed from Chimaltenango, the bus ride was long and for her expensive, and, most of all, the little money the family saved for the treatments ran out. On later visits to the clinic shots of streptomycin were reinstituted, but this time they gave no relief. Her "bug" had developed resistance to the drug.

It is time to review the story of tuberculosis in families like that of Luisa—for there are millions of Luisas about the countryside and about the globe. Tuberculosis, like cholera and some other life-threatening maladies, is generally a disease of poverty, afflicting the undernourished and spreading to waiting victims living in crowded quarters. Luisa's family is a classic example: eight people living in one small room with minimal food, the mother spewing tubercular bacilli over those in contact with her. Now she is infected again—or still.

In so far as Luisa's disease and inability to pay are problems of economic and social inequities, society might be held responsible for correcting the situation. However, the public sector, i.e., the government which presumably represents society, now lacks the resources, the wisdom and the infrastructure needed to deal with the many Luisas and their families. An alternative to public assistance is help from the private sector—therefore, she came to us. But our institution, like other private programs in poor communities, also confronts margins and cannot indefinitely take on a growing share of the societal responsibility. What to do?

Luisa's options are not only limited but also complicated. The only cash income for her home comes through seasonal work on the large plantations of the Pacific Coast lowlands which is characterized by a multitude of environmental and health problems. Her husband and the older boys return from coffee picking on the coast more malnourished than when they left and are often sick. They too must expend a major share of their income in getting well or lose their very ability to go to work. Thus, the poor get sicker and the sick get poorer in a downward spiral.

The Chimaltenango Development Program was conceived and born in the face of problems like Luisa's. It is dedicated not only to curing the sick but to initiating processes that touch more basic causes of sickness and health and turn the spiral upward.

A TWELVE-FOLD INCREASE FOR FELIX BALÁN   1971

The Maya of highland Guatemala depend almost entirely on their ability to make the land produce. A crop failure means that the head of the family may have to go to the coast to work for a pittance a day on other people's lands and expose himself to the dangers of intestinal parasites and malaria. It means that the man's wife may have to cut down the family's ration from one piece of meat a week to one piece a month or none at all. It also means, when one of the children gets sick, that the family gambles a few more days before their money is spent on a bus ride and a doctor's fees.

For Felix Balán a twelve-fold increase in his corn crop, achieved with the help of our agricultural co-workers over the last three years, means that he can set up a meat shop in a town of 8,000 people where meat has been available only two days of the week. For the people of Choatalum, soil improvement practices —including contour ditches, compost heaps, better cultivation and conservation of crop residues (previously burned) — have now helped raise the moisture-holding capacity of their soils to a point where, in addition to their recently quintupled corn harvests, they will be able to grow a high-value crop of tomatoes during the six-month dry season. For the people of Tioxa, the replacement of one harvest of low-value sugar cane with two to three harvests of tomatoes or chili peppers and two harvests of corn in the same period of time is changing the whole economy of the town.

Last year more than 700 soil analyses were performed by our workers with residents of more than 40 villages. New varieties of corn, beans and legumes were introduced to hundreds of farmers, new compost practices to even more, and a rotating loan fund benefited two hundred families. There are also ongoing activities for development of small industries, animal care, home improvement and family planning.

Such achievements, which become visible in the markets, are now bringing delegations of town leaders to our door asking for collaboration, whereas most programs find their biggest problem in getting people interested. This new confidence is attested by individuals like the one whose heroism I witnessed last weekend in Chidonjuán. Here was a villager who, as a result of new courage gained through collaboration, had decided he would no longer go to the coast, where he had repeatedly gotten sick. Instead he had spent forty-two solid days with a pick, axe and hoe preparing his little field in Chidonjuán for this year's crops!

MARÍA DE LA CRUZ HITS A PIG   1975

María de la Cruz hit a pig the other day while bringing a patient into the hospital in the ambulance jeep and had to pay the owner ten quetzals. This is nothing special — everyone hits a pig at one time or another. However, María is a Kaqchikel nurse who is the first young woman in the area to earn a license to drive a heavy-duty, four wheel drive vehicle. She took her driver training course up and down steep mountain tracks under the supervision of a very brave Peace Corps Volunteer. Now she wonders whether she has set back the progress of women, of health, and of her race. But of course she is setting all these forward.

THE WITH-IT YOUNG PRIEST   1975

A new young priest was assigned to Chimaltenango early this year and immediately set out to show leaders of the local *cofradía* (a religious fraternity combining Catholic elements with ancient Mayan patterns of worship and social structure) the error of their syncretistic ways. Matters became tense and the local police told newspaper reporters from Guatemala City that they were preparing for the worst.

Appeals were made to the bishop in Sololá. The priest defended his stand by announcing that this is the 20th century and that ancient ways must now be put aside. The bishop wisely transferred our up-to-date young priest. Peace has returned to the parish.

A MATTER OF LANGUAGE   1975

Rural people in Guatemala, our patients included, often simply step outside to relieve themselves. When they come to our hospital they bring with them all their habits, including this one. The local police became upset by human droppings that could be found almost every morning in the gutter in front of the hospital and in the alley behind. So the town council put up a sign saying that anyone using the gutter or alley in this fashion would be subject to a five quetzal fine.

One morning, a most indignant policeman brought the father of one of our patients inside the hospital bellowing that "this stupid Indian pig was stooling—right beneath the sign, no less!" I asked whether he had explained to the man what the sign said. The policeman replied that "this dumb bastard can't even speak Spanish." I suggested that he explain the sign to the man in Kaqchikel, the local Mayan language. The policeman replied rather sheepishly that he wasn't able to do that, and maybe it would just be better to forget the whole thing for now.

SPRING   1975

The dust is thick in Chimaltenango these days, like a Sahara sandstorm at times. If visitors complain that paving the streets would help, we say nicely, "Well, Chimaltenango's streets are made for feet, not for wheels."

The fields in highland Guatemala are bare and dry, waiting for the rains to come in May so planting can begin. The centuries-old cycle of corn cultivation will reawaken under the shadows of the great volcanos.

WINTER   1978

At 6:24 this morning as the sun slipped over the eastern edge of the earth it brushed the shrouded slope of Agua, the local water volcano. This ancient volcano fills with water and has burst in the past to enter unpredictably into modern history. Its brush by the sun, however, is as predictable as anything on earth. Agua lies due south-southeast of our house, so the sun in its journey northward is nearing Capricorn. The year must be nearly spent.

Might we reflect a bit on what time has brought to us here and to people elsewhere on the world scene? The human potential for illness and evil coming out in the jungles of Guyana and Brazil, inhuman social and political orders under tin-horn military dictators, the sinful consumerism and permissive lifestyles of industrial countries — these are indeed sorrows.

But making more sense of our program here in Chimaltenango by admitting faults, detecting paternalisms and inequities, then beginning anew the transformation process, and a growing global awareness that some existing social systems are indeed in need of change — these are the joys and bright spots one needs in order to carry on.

Child care on a farm of Las Mercedes.

A manifold increase for the farmer.

Institutions that historically have exploited humans seem now partly in decline. The plastic Jesuses, the phony professionals, the destroyers of nature, all are objects of suspicion and of new calls for accountability. Yet great dependencies remain—patients on doctors, parishioners on preachers, clients on lawyers, workers on industrialists, constituents on politicians, many poor on a few rich.

Hope and good sense, along with the pleasure of simply living together physically, humanly, socially and culturally—these one can find always and everywhere. They are the beginning of health.

When the sun makes its turn to journey back to the north, just before we celebrate the Star of Bethlehem and all it signifies, we in Chimaltenango will move through mixed thoughts to feeling good about the year gone by, about what now exists and about what the coming year might bring. We hope you, who share this work in many other places of the world, will do the same.

CHICKENS AND APPLES IN CHIPIACUL   1990

Chipiacul sits high on a plateau that looks alternately over the Pacific and the coastal plain, down on the ever-changing beauty of Lake Atitlán at the foot of its volcanos, and over to the valley of Iximché which was a cradle of Kaqchikel city-states in pre-Columbian days. In 1970 we initiated a program with the women of this village, where no services of any kind were available; but for reasons we did not then fully understand, it failed.

In 1973 we again visited Chipiacul with thoughts of reactivating a women's group devoted to health. This time, when the women came together, we told them we would like to work with them again but that nothing would be done until they had an opportunity to discuss this possibility with their husbands and neighbors. We knew that most of the children suffered from diarrhea, but we did not want to be the first to mention it.

A month later we returned and spoke with the women again. They did not say they wanted medicine for diarrhea. Instead they said, "All our chickens died." That was a serious problem for them because they were nine miles from the nearest market, which was held only once a week. Normally, chicken was their only source of meat, and new eggs were good for the children. They went on to say that they wanted to grow apples, which grew well at that altitude and could be sold profitably in the market. These then were the things they thought they needed—chickens and apples. Nothing else was discussed.

We promised to send them an agricultural extension worker who would show them how to build proper chicken houses and how to feed and immunize the chickens. Then, when the right time of year came around, he would help them plant apple trees. Nothing else.

Last summer I visited Chipiacul again. The village is transformed. During the intervening years a relationship of trust and cooperation has evolved. As the chickens and apple trees grew, the people came to recognize and address additional problems. They now have a full-time health promoter, a clinic, a good water supply, latrines in every home—a community infrastructure that would be the envy of any Guatemalan town.

Many health programs look good on paper but fail because they have been designed solely by professionals. It is different when the indigenous people work on their own terms, learn from their own failures and build on what they themselves have done. That is what "development" is all about.

5

THE CHIMALTENANGO
DEVELOPMENT PROGRAM

Carroll Behrhorst

1974, 1975, 1982

For the past nineteen years, I have lived and worked with the Kaqchikel of Guatemala—a proud, dignified, life-loving but impoverished people. Their cultural heritage stems from the Mayan civilization that lavished artistic, architectural and intellectual riches through the areas of Southern Mexico, Yucatán, Guatemala, Belize and Honduras many centuries before the Spanish conquest. I have gone to school with the Kaqchikel, letting them teach me—a North American doctor trained in the complex technology of modern medicine—the simplicities of what they believe is needed to live and prosper in the highlands of Guatemala. This is an area where nearly four million agrarian Maya now eke out a bare existence beneath the slumbering volcanoes that dominate this land of majestic beauty and sordid poverty.

I have learned more from my Mayan friends than they have learned from me, and I have come to believe that much of what I have absorbed here has application to the rural poor throughout the world. What I saw and heard in the course of surveys of mission hospitals in Africa and Asia confirmed my suspicion that basic problems in Guatemala are widely duplicated elsewhere. Despite important differences of culture, language and race, the rural poor of all continents share a commonality forged of poverty, exploitation, disease, malnutrition and land hunger.

As a result of my "student days" with the Kaqchikel and my travels among peoples facing similar problems, I have reached a number of conclusions concerning the great public health question of the day—how do they, how do we, how do they and we together break the back of disease among two billion rural poor in the less developed regions of the world? In 1962 when I arrived in Chimaltenango from a medical practice in Kansas, I would have said that curative medicine was the primary strategy. I have learned otherwise the hard way. This answer proved unrealistic both in terms of reaching by means of clinics and hospitals the ailing people in jungles, savannas and mountains, and in terms of keeping them healed when they return to the conditions which can fell them again within months, often within days, of their treatment.

Today the answer seems at once more simple and more complex. Impossible as the problem appears to many, I am now convinced that a fruitful beginning can be made by people outside the health bureaucracies of the world. I am also convinced that, with careful nurturing and persistence, an impact can be made from humble and inexpensive beginnings. I think we have proved this in Guatemala, although we still have a long, long way to go. Let me describe the origin and evolution of our experiment in the Guatemalan highlands.

These highlands are like many other areas of the "developing" world when seen through the lens of economic and public health statistics. They are predominantly agricultural and poor in cumulative resources. The wealth that exists is concentrated in the hands of an elite class. While the gross national product is increasing, largely through farm exports, the great mass of the people do not share in the benefits. The economic condition of the Kaqchikel is reflected in their state of health. The infant mortality rate is one of the highest in the world. Respiratory infections, malnutrition and intestinal disorders are primary causes of death; and many other diseases, such as measles, tuberculosis, whooping cough and influenza—no longer considered threats in the industrialized countries—still stalk the ridges and valleys.

This is one of the few areas in Latin America where the pre-Columbian population is still predominant. Mayan descendants make up more than three-fourths of the inhabitants of the highlands. They have held tenaciously to their culture and preserved their communities with a high degree of success. This requires that work with them be done on their own terms. While they are adapters, they have little appetite to copy modern cultures.

HOW THE PROJECT BEGAN

I came to Chimaltenango, a hub of the Guatemalan highlands, two decades ago under sponsorship of a Lutheran church body. During the first weeks I did little more than walk around town, get acquainted with the people and play with the children. Gradually, I was invited into their homes to have coffee with them or sit down to a meal of tortillas and beans. This went on for three months until I became known and accepted in the town and until I felt confident that I could fulfill a need.

That moment arrived when I accompanied a man, who was carrying a child's casket (not the first he had carried) to his home. Intravenous feeding mercifully turned back a case of prolonged diarrhea and extreme dehydration in his infant child. During the days that followed I practiced in the square, accompanied by a nurse recruited from Guatemala City who helped train local women as aides. Then I rented a house for $25 a month and opened a clinic. The first day 125 patients came. I was in the business of curing.

It did not take long to realize that I was trying to empty an ocean of disease and malfunction with a medical teaspoon. While this is not the place to analyze my personal transformation, let me illustrate a fundamental change that took place in my thinking and attitudes by recounting what happened to Jorge.

I met Jorge about a year after coming to Chimaltenango. He was a handsome five-year-old boy but he was suffering that day he came to the clinic with his mother. He had puffy eyes, swollen feet, pigmentation blemishes on his arms and legs and stains the color of port wine. I found that he lived in the village of San Jacinto in the rugged mountain country near Chimaltenango. Since he was not the first child from San Jacinto to come with this problem, I decided to go to the town for a look at conditions there.

I drove by jeep to San Jacinto with two women helpers. Though the village is only five miles from Chimaltenango, the journey was a long one. There was no road at that time and our wheels often became mired in mud holes. At last we left the vehicle and walked the rest of the way. The trouble in San Jacinto was not hard to diagnose. Almost every child we saw was malnourished and diarrhea was common in both adults and children. A great deal of coughing could be heard. As we visited the thatch-roofed huts we learned that the common diet included very little protein. The village lived almost exclusively on tortillas and greens.

Why? The people had no land to farm, only miserable little plots in areas where the soil was poor. San Jacinto was almost completely surrounded by large plantations operated for the benefit of absentee owners. The men of the village, seeking to earn a bare living, customarily packed up once a year and went to work on the big coffee fincas on the Pacific coast. Going from the cool highlands to the hot lowlands they fell victim to a variety of tropical ailments and many returned to the village with tuberculosis. When the two nurses from our clinic made a house-to-house survey they found that 150 of the 450 residents had active tuberculosis.

We realized that, no matter how many times we treated Jorge and other youngsters from San Jacinto, they would never be healthy until basic changes were made in the village. We began

Returning with the day's harvest from a field near Santa María de
Jesús.

in a simple, tentative way. A Peace Corps volunteer attached to the clinic made weekly visits to San Jacinto, gained the confidence of the men and began to teach better farming methods to a group who tilled their plots for survival.[1] Later, we lent money from our initial operating funds to twenty-five families who wished to raise chickens and produce eggs. Soon the people began to eat more protein — "an egg a day" became a slogan in the village. The loan was repaid in full, the borrowers giving us a portion of their egg production in lieu of cash.

Gradually our work expanded in San Jacinto. A Kaqchikel health worker who trained with us in Chimaltenango opened his own small clinic in the village and began treating the most common ailments on a fee-for-service basis. On request of the villagers, native extension workers of the Chimaltenango program taught health care, nutrition and farming methods. Ten families banded together and bought some land held by an absentee owner, borrowing from our operating fund and paying us back conscientiously as crops began to bring a dribble of cash to the town. Year by year, more land was purchased with the help of a revolving land-loan fund, which was set up with the aid of grants from international foundations. The women of the village organized a weaving and marketing club which brought more income than the handful of coins they had formerly gained through individual efforts.

Today San Jacinto is a reasonably healthy, economically viable community. Malnutrition has all but disappeared and the dreaded tuberculosis has been controlled. You can walk through the village today without hearing much coughing. Jorge himself is a robust young man. While San Jacinto is still poor, it has a new vibrancy compounded of protein, cash, work and hope.

True, San Jacinto is not the world, but a million San Jacintos might transform the world. As our program evolved, we came to see dozens of San Jacintos in the Guatemalan highlands and came to feel that we were on the right track. In brief, what started as curing the sick broadened into a general community program

---

[1] This was Wayne Haag, author of chapter 17 in this volume, "Features of Effective Agricultural Programs in Ghana and Other Lands."

geared to activities that the residents want and need and that result in self-empowerment.

These experiences have hammered home a strategic truth. Institutionalized charity from outside accomplishes little beyond the cosseting of the egos of the helpers. The Kaqchikel receive no charity from us. They pay for the services they want, borrow at reasonable interest rates, and select the people who are to work with them. All of our health promoters are Maya, as are most of our nurses and extension workers. The clinical staff now includes two Guatemalan doctors, one of whom serves as the medical director. If we outsiders do not plan ways of doing ourselves out of a job we are probably not doing the job at all.

The Chimaltenango program never abandoned curative medicine. Indeed, without curing, our expanded program would have been difficult to initiate or to sustain. However, changes were required even in our medical practice. During the early years our work was subsidized by a Lutheran church body and we also had access to some free and discount medicines. If these arrangements were to continue indefinitely, however, the local people would become dependent on outside aid that is not entirely reliable. During our first years, moreover, we were able to deal with infectious diseases on an outpatient basis through antibiotics, electrolyte solutions and immunizations. But as word spread, many more sick people began arriving. Some came from great distances, sometimes on the back of a porter, and were too ill to make the long, hard journey home. So we had both to intensify our curative services and to adjust familiar medical practices.

THE HOSPITAL

Conventional hospitals are a very expensive proposition. Poor rural areas cannot afford the hotel services and elaborate facilities of modern hospitals. Moreover, impressive buildings with sophisticated rules of procedure are almost certain to alienate people who are used to being cared for by family members.

Already in 1962, as demands grew in Chimaltenango, we decided to build a very modest hospital with a difference. Here families could stay with their patients and would be responsible for preparing food and providing basic care. This arrangement turned out to be not only far less expensive but also far more humane. Costs to the patient in our hospital, including all services and medicine, now work out to about three dollars per day. This payment does not cover all our expenses, but that is because we accept any and all patients regardless of their ability to pay and because unequal ancillary services like transport are funded from the general budget.

Though the hospital enabled us to treat more patients for longer periods of time, there were still many people living at great distances who could not afford to travel to Chimaltenango and many others who remained suspicious even of the modest "modern" services we offered. Here we faced a new set of problems. Having reformulated the concept of "hospital," we now challenged that of "doctor" as well.

HEALTH PROMOTERS

As a medical professional I was at first disposed to think of duplicating the functions of the medical physician in medically deficient communities by creating mini-doctors who would provide services patterned after those offered in Chimaltenango. I then discovered that this device of dispatching mini-doctors would not prove acceptable, given the high suspicion that prevails on the part of the people with respect to impositions from outside their own community and culture. Moreover, such service delivery might diminish the multiple initiatives that are needed on the part of the people themselves. A new type of community worker had to be created, one that was not patterned after the doctor but was rather a product of the community itself.

During the first years of seeing 125 to 200 patients a day, we began to realize that a bright Kaqchikel, given a certain amount of inexpensive training, could treat the most common diseases just as well as a university-trained doctor. Not only would the investment of time and finance be far more modest, but the ability to work in accordance with the customs of the people could prove

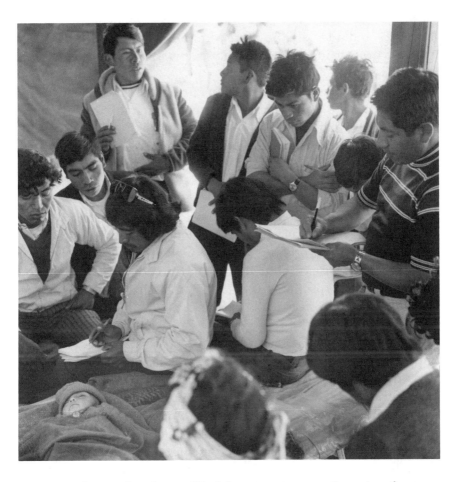

Training day at the clinic. Health promoters are learning from an infant.

invaluable in pursuing community arrangements for health and in gaining acceptance of some unfamiliar medicines and procedures. From the mid-1960s we began training responsible young Maya to recognize and alleviate the most common health problems. This program grew to include more than seventy health promoters from fifty villages.

Although the formal education of our promoters had ended, on average, after the third grade of elementary school, they were for the most part alert, eager to learn and quite skillful at treating ailments within their competence. One day we took an American specialist in tropical medicine on a tour of the health promoters at work. He was skeptical that persons with little formal education could administer adequate medical care, but as the day wore on and he saw promoters dealing knowledgeably with one ailment after another, his skepticism abated. Finally, he thought he had caught one of the promoters giving an incorrect treatment. "You have the right disease, but the wrong remedy," he said to the promoter. "The specific indicated here is penicillin." The young Kaqchikel shook his head. "Yes," he replied, "but this person is allergic to penicillin."

The manner in which trainees came to be selected is of critical importance. At first we accepted those who were recommended to us by a local priest or a Peace Corps volunteer. In two cases local curanderos, who practiced traditional healing, elected to enlarge their service by becoming promoters in our program. Later our approach was to encourage each community to set up a local improvement council, which included a health committee. Then the community health committee selected a person for training. The promoter thus represented his community and was also accountable to the community. In cases of discipline, the community could decide to retain him or recommend his dismissal.

As part of their training, health promoters are asked to come once a week to Chimaltenango and spend an entire day with us. Their day begins with hospital rounds in the company of a doctor or supervisor. They see patients, hear the interviews and observe the treatments, then give consideration to how those very problems could be handled—and prevented—in their home villages. We usually do not speak of diseases by name but rather talk of the patient's symptoms, since symptoms have meaning to the people while classifications do not. I wish to emphasize my belief that any program for training lay workers that does not include facilities for demonstration with patients cannot be effective. A living demonstration accomplishes as much as six hours of lectures. Films, books, pamphlets and seminars are adjuncts but no substitutes for this.

Our program of health promoter training is a continuing one. Before a promoter dispenses medicines or gives injections, he has attended observation and reflection sessions for at least a year. Nearly all promoters, even those who began their training more than ten years before, return on a regular basis to gain new insights and observe treatments. We conduct periodic reviews in which promoters are asked to describe what they see in a patient, how they would proceed with the patient, and what is to be done in the patient's home and village to prevent a recurrence in the future. Promoters are visited on the job by a supervisor, an experienced Mayan worker, who is in charge of the program.

Although they identify and treat most diseases in their communities and work with as many as a thousand patients a year, there are some medical tasks that are beyond the competence of the health promoters. They are trained to recognize these and to make referrals to the clinic in Chimaltenango or to another nearby health center. For example, an elderly man with swollen feet and shortness of breath probably has heart disease. The promoter is responsible for seeing that this sufferer receives professional help, even if it means carrying him out of the village in a chair tied to a porter's back. Generally, on the basis of such understandings, the promoters do very well (Muller 1977).

Promoters do not carry drugs with potentially serious side effects, such as corticosteroids and digitalis preparations. Given this limitation and firm agreements against overuse, the buying and selling of medicines is carried on in a businesslike way. Our clinic places the orders for common medicines in Guatemala City, since we can buy at reduced hospital prices. All supplies are then passed to a promoters' medicine cooperative at our price plus a 10 percent handling fee. The medicine cooperative, in turn, sells directly to the promoters at the co-op's purchase price plus 10 percent for its expenses. Thus, medicine is available to promoters and their patients at reduced prices, much below those quoted by the pharmacies.

Each local health committee receives a price list for medicines and the promoter is expected to charge accordingly. In addition, promoters may charge a fee of 50 cents for their call or services. The profit motive naturally affects their attitude toward their job, but they are not expected or encouraged to make a livelihood from their medical practice. They are, without exception, more secure financially than they were before training, while rendering a service never before performed in their village. No promoter receives any pay from the parent organization in Chimaltenango.

Since the promoters generally work with poverty-stricken people, some of whom cannot afford to pay cash, they have developed a system of credit that is both effective and reliable. The success of this system derives in part from the culture of the highland peoples. Responsibility, respect and honesty belong to the local tradition.

In addition to the curing aspects of their labors, health promoters become community catalysts and organizers. They educate with respect to family nutrition and foster community provisions for health. Immunizations, tuberculosis control and treatment, water projects, literacy programs, family planning, agricultural extension, introduction of fertilizers, new crops and better seeds, chicken projects, improved animal husbandry—all may come into the promoter's purview.

AGRICULTURAL EXTENSION SERVICE

A natural outgrowth of our work in health promotion was agricultural extension work, which we began in 1966. The people of the Guatemalan highlands are mostly farmers. By tradition the staples of their diet are corn and vegetables, particularly beans. A farmer must raise sufficient corn to supply his family with tortillas from one harvest to the next. If the harvest is poor, their livelihood is directly threatened.

An agricultural extensionist tests the soil with farmers at Patzaj.

But the typical farmer is land poor. Land holdings, already small, become further fractionated as the Mayan farmer, in accordance with tradition, divides his holdings equally among his sons. There are, however, a significant number of large estates that are left fallow by indifferent absentee owners, who maintain title only because of prestige or family tradition or as an investment. Some people live on these estates as tenant farmers.

Help is available to these farmers through extension agronomists who have received training in government-sponsored programs or from senior workers in our program. Our agricultural extension activities initially concentrated on obvious measures — use of fertilizers, better seeds, soil improvement, crop diversification including vegetables and cold-weather fruits, introduction and improvement of chickens, veterinary medicine and similar strategies that help the subsistence farmer produce more nourishing food for himself and his family. Many farmers have increased their yields two to three times and, in some cases, improvements have been even more dramatic.

Our program has remained tentative and flexible with respect to the use of manufactured agricultural accessories. Large mechanical implements, such as tractors, are less attractive here because of the rugged terrain and the cost of buying and maintaining machinery. We have, however, been strongly tempted by some chemical fertilizers. These have been introduced after analysis of soil samples and have definitely improved yields. Today, however, because of a worldwide shortage of manufactured fertilizers and a consequent rise in price, we are once again reminded of the hazards of relying on outside technology. Just as our medical approach must emphasize disease prevention, thereby releasing people from dependence on manufactured pharmaceuticals, so must our agricultural efforts stress implements and resources that the people can supply themselves. Accordingly, our program has increased experimentation with composts and natural fertilizers that control the balance of elements in the soil.

The primary limitation on innovations is the poverty of the average small farmer, who does not have ready money to invest in experiments. He finds loans extremely difficult to obtain or available only from a private money-lender who charges an intolerable rate of interest. To meet this need, the program has set up a revolving fund to provide farmers with credit on easy terms for specific agricultural projects. Gradually this revolving loan fund is being replaced by a local agricultural savings and loan cooperative that is managed and controlled by the people themselves.

THE LAND LOAN PROGRAM (ULEU)

The most formidable obstacle to the success of our agricultural work has been the shortage or inequitable distribution of land. Indeed, land hunger is at the root of almost every major problem in these Guatemalan highlands. We have noted how farmers who own no land or only a piece too small to meet family needs are forced to migrate seasonally to the tropical coffee and cotton plantations of the Pacific slopes. There they receive low wages, live in squalid conditions, aggravate the primary health problems of infectious disease and malnutrition—and lose time they might otherwise spend improving crop yields in their own highland village.

Moreover, when farmers do not own a suitable piece of land in the highlands or share in land ownership through a collective, they have scant incentive to improve the soil. Were they to introduce extensive conservation measures by building terraces and contour ditches or using fertilizers and a simpler plow, the yield and value of the land would rise and the owner would demand more rent —possibly pricing the farmers out of the very land they have improved. As a result, many farmers refuse to employ techniques they know would improve land yields.

Responding to this dilemma, we established in 1970 a program to make loans available to communities of Mayan farmers who wish to buy their own land. Loans are made only to groups, since large purchasers enjoy a better bargaining position and since this will reduce the cost of extension services. Our revolving loan fund program is called ULEU, a Kaqchikel word for "land," and is governed by a board of directors composed of extensionists and representatives of the cooperatives—all local people. The loans are long-term with low interest rates by Guatemalan standards. The farmers do their own negotiating with the owners or former landlords to determine a sale price and payment plan.

We by no means suggest that this is a sufficient approach to the historical and deep-seated issues of land reform. But it is a good option for a voluntary group that undertakes to discover what people can do if they have the opportunity and if they undertake to work together. We hope to show that land reform can prove very effective when it is taken up by a community and supported by a complex of skills and capacities. We also hope to demonstrate how closely land reform is tied to public health.

WOMEN'S PROGRAMS

When first established, our agricultural extension program was oriented toward men, since it is they who work in the fields. Many health problems, however, are associated with activities around the home. With this in mind, we began in 1972 to train experienced Kaqchikel women who would travel to various villages demonstrating and encouraging aspects of household health such as nutrition and hygiene, sewing, home gardens and chicken projects. Because these extensionists were Mayan women who spoke the Kaqchikel tongue and wore the typical garb, they have been successful communicators.

Family planning is a part of this activity, though it is approached with sensitivity and respect for local traditions. The Mayan culture is dedicated to family, God and the earth; it does not take readily to limiting life or distorting nature. The people are suspicious of outsiders who come with the suggestion that they should limit their numbers. We should remind ourselves in the industrialized countries that each new child in the Guatemalan highlands will use during its lifetime only a tiny fraction of the irreplaceable natural resources (oil, iron, aluminum, etc.) that a child born in the United States will use. It requires 26 tons of ore to sustain the average citizen of the United States, compared with a fraction of a ton for the average Mayan resident of Guatemala.

Family planning sessions, offered exclusively by Kaqchikel women, do not bluntly raise the subject of birth control nor move

Women's program at Xajaxac, Sololá.   On the wall: "A child is a treasure."

quickly to showing what can be done with a particular apparatus, pill or injection. Rather, our workers sit down with a family and consider with them their own views of the situation. Any technicalities wait until the family is fully involved in the decision making on its own terms. Since the family makes the decision, the drop-out rate is low.

The people want positive results, not merely a limitation of offspring. They know that half their children now die of diseases linked with malnutrition. They want to know that those who follow them will have land and food. Thus, agricultural extension, nutrition advice and land reform programs all become integral parts of family planning.

WATER PROGRAMS

Lack of potable water has been a persistent health hazard in the highlands. In 1979, to combat this problem, we joined forces with the Guatemalan Ministry of Health and with Agua del Pueblo, an institution dedicated to improving sanitation and water resources. Together we formed SARUCH (Servicios de Agua Rural de Chimaltenango), an organization which works to increase supplies of pure water. The people receive loans to install not pumps but gravity-type systems, which are not subject to energy and mechanical problems.

It should be emphasized that these are more than "water projects," deposited on communities. They are, rather, a mobilization of people to address their most basic need and an excellent point of departure for dealing with the whole panorama of health-related problems. The people are themselves in charge of gaining participation, planning, forming objectives, managing the work and repaying loans.

This mobilizing dynamic becomes visible as children carry the pipes, men volunteer days away from their farming to dig the space for holding tanks and trenches for the kilometers of pipes which must be laid. On the great days of inauguration, entire villages rejoice in the gift of water and in the utility which they themselves have built.

A woman begins the long walk to fetch water from a mountain top near Xola, Quiché.

PROGRAM EVALUATION

Having reviewed the course of our program to here, we might wish to ask: What in fact has been accomplished? What are the strengths of the program and what are its shortcomings? Unfortunately, few comprehensive studies have been made and baseline data, which might later have served for comparative purposes, were not always collected. Given limited resources, we used what we had to help people, not to make measurements. Nonetheless, several outside evaluations have been undertaken and their criticisms have been instructive.

According to one report, written by a Canadian nurse in 1978, we were falling short in our pursuit of a primary objective. "The chief flaw which I observed in the otherwise excellent program was the fact that Dr. Behrhorst was still personally treating all the outpatients that came to the hospital" (Bent 1978). This was a largely valid complaint and one that we have struggled to correct. If programs like ours do not take root in native soil under local direction, they will wither the moment the foreign helpers cease their aid. We have now taken the steps, both legal and organizational, to assure that the program will be governed by a local board and administered by local staff on their own terms. The program is licensed as a private agency under Guatemalan law, with all policy matters in the hands of a local board of directors.

Another criticism, despite our best intentions, is a lingering overuse of drugs. Like the medical system itself, we have tended to rely too heavily on pharmaceutical preparations in the healing process. We have taken several corrective steps: we are restricting drug use to a limited list, substituting explanation for medication wherever possible and making better use of local herbal remedies.

Our clinical efforts have been criticized for their lack of support services and controls. Treatments are administered on the basis of clinical practice and are not always backed up by more sophisticated laboratory testing. There is some merit to this complaint, and we are improving our laboratory procedures and record-keeping. However, we remain convinced that the most important factor in the healing process is the patient, not records documenting the condition.

The work of our health promoters has proved gratifying in many ways, but even here we have had some problems. There are risks involved in placing medical responsibilities and tools in human hands, whether in Boston or in Comalapa. At times promoters have overtreated or overcharged their patients or have not dedicated themselves to total community efforts. For the most part, however, careful supervision by senior staff has prevented excesses of this kind. If, moreover, a promoter does not maintain acceptable standards of treatment and care, the community can discipline him or the medicine cooperative can refuse to sell him medicines.

Some outside observers have called into question the "capitalistic" practice of charging patients on a fee-for-service basis, suggesting that the community at large should pay for health services, not the individual. This sounds attractive but it would not work at present in the Guatemalan highlands. The Kaqchikel are skilled traders with an acute business sense, who believe that anything worthwhile must be earned and paid for. Public sector charity programs have met with little success here. Given these considerations, direct payment by the patient to the healer seems the preferred system, with the special provision of a credit system and use of the Robin Hood principle — charging slightly higher fees to those who can afford to pay and considerably lower fees to the very poor.

Most observers have been impressed by the integral approach taken by our program (Glittenberg 1974, Heggenhougen 1976). In areas where our extension workers have been active there is direct evidence of crop improvement, more cash income, less malnutrition and infectious disease, improved hygiene and sanitation, cleaner and more available water, and a greater number of immunized children. The land and agricultural loan programs have had the additional positive effects of freeing farmers from the need to migrate to the plantations of the south coast. What they require for their livelihood they are now producing on their own land.

References

Bent, Muriel F.
    1978 The Role of Auxiliary Health Workers in the Delivery of
          Primary Health Care. Ottawa: International Development
          Research Centre.
Glittenberg, JoAnn
    1974 Adapting Health Care to a Cultural Setting. American
          Journal of Nursing (December).
Heggenhougen, H. Kris
    1977 Health Care for the "Edge of the World" — Indian Cam-
          pesinos as Health Workers in Chimaltenango, Guatemala: A
          Discussion of the Behrhorst Program. New York:
          Dissertation to New School of Social Research.
Muller, Frederik
    1979 Participación Popular en Programas de Atención Sanitaria
          Primaria en América Latina. Pp. 124-35. Medillín:
          Universidad de Antioquia.

6

THE EARTH'S UNDOING

Carroll Behrhorst

This dawn marks the two-week anniversary of the earth's undoing here in highland Guatemala. Communications have been sparse, as you all know. Day before yesterday the mail came for the first time. Now time and circumstance allow this note to you. It is not possible to write something to each of you personally, so I am asking letter writers of the Embassy Wives to copy this out and send it to you all.

Where to begin? First let me say that my family and I are in excellent straits, both in body and spirit. We have legs on which to move about—this cannot be said of friends who are now lying, still forever, in a large trench gouged by a bulldozer for the many

77

dead, or of those who will never move a leg again because of hard blows to the back from falling beams and adobe blocks.

We were asleep when it happened. I woke when the house beams stopped their creaking and waving about. My son had leapt out of bed to run outside but fell in a large pile of plates which gashed his face. We both quickly pulled on our pants and headed for town. When we reached the bottom of our hill, it became obvious that the destruction was extensive — not one home on the road stood higher than a human head. Streets were impassable because of large heaps of rubble. Almost every house we passed had lost family members. We made our way to the center of the town where we found the clinic and hospital — which had been built against the eventuality of an earthquake — still intact and all the patients uninjured. The night nurse had broken her arm when, in haste, she tried to force the door. She was the only casualty among our workers, though the nurses from outlying villages lost many family members.

We went quickly to the homes of the local nurses to see if there were any injuries, but miraculously there were none. I then returned to the clinic to prepare for the deluge of patients that would arrive once dawn appeared. Characteristically, within an hour almost all the Kaqchikel nurses were on duty and ready to work, though I must admit that our Ladino workers were not so responsive and some were days in showing up. This traces to their culture, in that they tend to think of themselves and immediate family first, while the Maya relate to the broader community around them. When light finally appeared in the east, the true extent of the tragedy became apparent. No need to repeat this, since you have seen it on your television screens. Most towns in this area of the highlands are completely destroyed.

We all, of course, have death and destruction about us all the time in various forms, seen and unseen, but it usually does not come in such great bunches. Many have asked, how did you respond to it all? The answer is simple. A great deal of learning has come from my Mayan friends. I now view life as an experience from day to day, knowing that into each day enter joy, sorrow, exhilaration, defeat and frustration, that all these have a place, and that one responds positively, doing what must be done to make the day meaningful. In the dawn hours following the first big shake, I told the assembled health workers that obviously there was much to do, that chaotic behavior heaped on a chaotic situation had no place in what we all needed to do now, and that good sense, good humor and faith were essential as in all situations. They responded well, unusually well, particularly the Kaqchikel staff who understand life and tragedy better than we do.

How does the foundation fit into this vast happening? Throughout the disaster we have tried to maintain normalcy. Great flexibility has been necessary, of course, and hard decisions have been made about what needs doing and what must be left undone. When, two days later, the second earthquake damaged the outpatient and extension offices beyond repair, our entire program became centered in the hospital building. Since we are the only full-time hospital facility in the entire department, the bulk of work continues to fall on our small staff. I believe we are up to it. Hundreds of volunteers have appeared on the scene, but most of these have now left and we are down to our usual staff, including Peace Corps workers and medical students from New York.

Many pages could be filled in telling the local story, but I believe it is time to get to work and do what needs doing in the usual way. We send hasty good wishes and love to all.

P.S. Since our house was of the same construction as the hospital, it was scarcely damaged. There are a few cracks, plaster has fallen in and some tiles have slipped — so you can sit in the bathroom and see the sky. At such times one can also make a short reflection.

> Now that my house has fallen down
> I have a much better view of the moon.

[FROM A TAPED COMMUNICATION]   UNDATED

Our first concern was to line up the various types of medicines and supplies that we thought we'd need when the people started arriving. So we cleared away debris and set up a series of stations. First was a sorting station for filling out charts, when possible, giving the names of patients, their towns, their injuries and the treatments indicated. Then four treatment stations—for obvious fractures, for lacerations, for people near death, and for people who were least injured. Persons needed to be identified quickly, then cared for in the most immediate way with the limited resources we had at hand.

People started coming around 4:30 in the morning and we were ready. When the sun climbed over the wall, people arrived in large numbers. People who had formerly come to us as patients now brought injured family members, neighbors and friends.

Most people had fractures. I have never before seen such an astonishing number and array of broken bones at one time. I am now told that 55,000 people suffered fractures during that half-minute quake. A doctor in Denver informs me that never in recorded medical history have more fractures been incurred in a single day, not even during times of war.

This, of course, posed problems. People came with bones sticking out of their arms, legs and chest, with beams running through torsos and sticking into bellies, and with the most bizarre and horrendous wounds imaginable. In spite of our attempt to keep records, we don't really have a good count. I suppose we saw between 600 and 700 cases in the first forty-eight hours.

Our Mayan nurses worked almost steadily for two days and two nights, and I alongside them. During that time it was difficult to get any assistance from the outside because the roads were blocked. With the opening of the roads, help came not only from Guatemala City but from Nicaragua and elsewhere. A large army field hospital arrived from Oklahoma, equipped to care for those needing surgery. I wish to report that the gringos did very well, kept their work and image at low key and collaborated well with other nationals, including Hondurans, Nicaraguans and Mexicans. For that matter, I heard a number of journalists say they had never seen the Guatemalan military people respond in such a positive way—in contrast to many criticisms of Latin American military establishments.

JULY 27, 1976

The earthquake and its disruptions are over but, of course, there remain all about us reminders of the devastation and losses that came on February 4. As I have often said, the local people are very resilient and have high tolerance for disorders of all sorts, since these are accepted within the context of natural happenings. So even after a violent earthquake there was a search for constructive responses, not remorse and loss of will because of tragedy. Within hours of the destruction there was a general concern that some sense of normalcy should be achieved and that has been the dominant theme ever since.

Reconstruction has proceeded along lines that reflect the history of highland Guatemala, where life has been physically marginal for centuries and where it is necessary to make do with what is at hand for survival. Galvanized and wooden materials have been supplied for cover, and more permanent construction is now taking place. The warmth and color of the tile and adobe have mostly disappeared from the landscape, because even the mud that the poor were able to mold with their own hands has now brought injury and death. Crops generally were not damaged, so farming goes on. In fact, we are having a quite encouraging rainy season with better than average yields in store.

The program here in Chimaltenango is back to its usual priorities, though in crowded quarters since the extension complex had to be razed. New construction is under way, thanks to many old and new friends, and we will have a useful facility up within eight or nine months.

Here I should like to focus on our goals for this year. While they extend beyond the context of the earthquake, it would be nonsense to assume the quake did not upset and revise some scheduling and operations. I here wish to mention several objectives that are high priorities before us now. They are all part and parcel of our general purpose to stand beside the people as best we may on their terms, putting knowledge, tools and decision making in their hands. Involvement by foreigners, self-fulfillment by "serving" individuals and institutions, and the excesses of pro-

New extension complex under construction.

fessionals are all being kept at a lowest possible key. This year's objectives include the following.

Dependence on local resources, both human and material, are to be achieved absolutely.

This demands a phasing out of foreigners, and I have at hand a flow-and-phase-out chart that shows no non-Guatemalan on the staff within five years from now, except for one or two in rather distant advisory functions (myself included).   The increasing interest income from revolving funds will help substantially in meeting the budget. If we can divest ourselves of the overweening sin of pharmaceutical products and thereby lower drug costs we will be on the way to sustaining the total program through local income.

Health will be served as much as possible outside the context and concept of pills and injections.

Our curing programs, like those around the globe, are too heavily dependent on the use of drugs, which are produced and delivered by expansive and exploitative businesses. The local peoples cannot afford the excesses of drug researchers and drug makers (nor, for that matter, can the people in Princeton, New Jersey). Along with the monopoly of the medical profession, the power and mystique of the medicine manufacturers must be challenged. Local, home-type drug preparation must become a reality to bypass the distant pill makers.

Community workers will be just that.

Health auxiliaries are to assist the community in ways that give attention to the various interrelated social, economic, political and cultural factors. They must become aware of the epidemiological implications of every health problem and proceed on that basis to facilitate local solutions. Few societies can any longer afford the excesses and limited scope of the strictly medical curers, whether they be sophisticated physicians or physician assistants or paramedical people or physician extenders or whatever name is given to additional dispensers of curing-type services.

We have just finished an evaluation of our health promoters and too many of them are acting like mini-docs. Their role is still too limited, as is that of the doctor in Springfield or Silver Springs. A major objective this year is a complete revamping of the health training program to prepare human healers, not just curers. I can say with considerable pleasure that in a newer satellite program in Uspantán in the northern part of the country this has been achieved to a remarkable degree. Primary awareness is focused realistically on community perceptions and capacities. Objectives are formed by the community and are implemented through their functioning committee and their chosen health promoter. That is as it should be.

The concept of community involvement is to be articulated and implemented in a functional fashion.

In my experience even "community nuts" (and I consider myself one of these) really do not have an adequate perception of what genuine community involvement implies and entails. The concept is essential, but to meaningfully articulate it, formulate it, organize and implement it — that leaves a whole lot to be desired. Early next year I plan to visit some programs in Asia that are supposed to be exemplary.

Thanks to all of you who have given personal and group support to us here, particularly in the difficult days after the February catastrophe.

SEPTEMBER 8, 1976

First, something very important. I admit error in not expanding and clarifying my comments about "making our own drugs." As happens sometimes, I did not make room for qualifying details. We do, of course, need to reduce our costs as best we can, but we do not wish to do so at the expense of quality in our work with people. Need I remind us all of why we are in business—to support the patient and the community? Drug bills add a big bulge to our budget and we must do everything possible to reduce these costs—including getting people unhooked from drugs. However, we do not cut corners by producing drugs of inferior quality and then pretend we are saving money.

What we plan to do is to make every effort to mix locally those most needed medicines that can be compounded readily and safely in our own laboratory. We have the collaboration of the College of Pharmacy in this project, which will guarantee quality control through the presence of their own personnel in the production line. We wish to begin by preparing several simple solutions, including diarrhea mixtures and cough expectorants.

Groups, including Church World Service, are interested in making funds available for water projects and small agricultural loans. Potentially large sums of money are involved. Now we do, of course, wish to convey funds, tools and other resources to communities—but always within the context of local realities. This entails a provision that all funds be available as loans, not grants, and that community responsibility be an integral part of any loan program. The way to such responsibility includes consciousness raising, appropriate extension services and development of adequate management. Because of this we are moving slowly, taking time to achieve the collaboration of all interested groups in an area, and are making certain there is proper coordination. Nothing can be more damaging to a community than improperly guided or mismanaged loan funds.

All this demands staff that have a sound community identity and good communication with local farmers, along with administrative skills. Such creatures generally do not exist, for persons with experience and sophisticated skills often do not relate well to the rural people, even if they are from a native background, and those who relate well to their own people often lack administrative skills. If we had limitless copies of our present extensionists, there would be no problem—but we have yet to find such people outside the program.

I mention this since there will probably be questions why we do not rush to accept the rather large amounts of funds that are potentially available at this time. The answer, now as always, is that we will accept money as we can properly use it.

A contrary example: In spite of all the good intentions and presumed understanding, the new aluminum roofing is a bust. No one in particular is to blame, but this initiative does reflect the old paternalism — a decision was made at the top to define and address people's needs without consulting them. There will be losses on the project since the roofing is not acceptable to local people because of its odd appearance, its high price and its tendency to keep out neither cold nor heat. Not one health promoter is interested in either buying or selling it.

7

THE VIOLENCE

Carroll Behrhorst

THE CONFLICTS IN GUATEMALA AS THEY BEAR ON THE CHIMALTENANGO DEVELOPMENT PROGRAM (MAY 8, 1981)

Recent intense political conflicts in the Chimaltenango area have interrupted program activities, even to the point of the kidnapping and killing of program workers. Although our work is explicitly apolitical and dedicated to a middle-of-the-road course in behalf of its mission, it is also clear to us that political goals are relevant to health. Lest any forget, disease has definite economic and social etiologies, so an overall strategy may demand political interventions as well as medical remedies. To imagine otherwise would be as foolhardy as to imagine that military strategies all by themselves are sufficient to resolve problems that have rooted economic and social causes.

Because of its community activities, the Chimaltenango program has become affected by the local political conflict. Community action, whether by social, educational, religious or development groups, has been viewed by government security forces as sowing seeds of "subversion." Hundreds of private and public workers have come under suspicion, but those fostering community action have been seen in particular as supportive of the guerrilla movement in the local countryside. Eight of our program workers have thus far been threatened or killed, or have disappeared and are presumed dead. People living in the communities served by these workers are often convinced that the kidnappers were with the government forces. In one case an army commander admitted as much in response to an inquiry by a health promoter.

Local Guatemalan newspapers testify to violence and excesses in various areas of the highlands, particularly in the Department of Chimaltenango. Massacres of dozens of people in nearby villages have been confirmed. Since investigations of these events are seldom forthcoming, there can be only speculation and rumor as to who is guilty of particular gross excesses. Both government forces and guerrilla elements are accused of brutality and atrocities.

In mid-March, 1981, letters were received by Guatemalan social institutions (reportedly five in number) indicating that the recipient agencies were staffed by "communists" and that all staff must leave the country within thirty days or suffer the consequences. The following week letters were sent to private voluntary institutions engaged in development work. These letters said that all foreigners involved in program efforts must leave the country or be "eliminated." Both groups of letters were signed by "Ejército Secreto Anti-Comunista," the "Secret Anti-Communist Army."

The Behrhorst Clinic was included in the second listing along with Church World Service, the Mennonites, Roman Catholics engaged in the agricultural program in San Lucas Tolimán, and some Norwegian groups. All of these agencies have relations with the Comité Nacional de Reconstrucción (National Committee for Reconstruction) and internationally with various funding groups.

Several days later, recipients of this letter were called to the office of the chief of the Comité, who told us that the letters were really a *locura* (a folly or absurdity), that the intent may have been to threaten the Comité itself. A consensus, shared by board members of the local Behrhorst Foundation, is that these letters had their origin within a reactionary sector of the government and were intended as a tool to destabilize and demoralize non-governmental institutions that have been involved in community work, particularly in the departments of Chimaltenango, Sololá and Quiché.

The government security forces are determined to control the countryside and eliminate the guerrilla movement at all costs. Any programs or individuals are suspect that do not collaborate with the government, especially if they are supportive of community efforts in areas of guerrilla activity. In terms of this mentality, all individuals and groups devoted to community action must either be controlled or else eliminated.

THE CHIMALTENANGO DEVELOPMENT PROGRAM
—ITS EVOLUTION 1961 TO 1982 (FROM A 1982 DRAFT)

It is appropriate here to discuss briefly the role of health promoters with respect to their function and future in communities involved in political conflict and civil war. These health workers assume the role of change agents in dealing with basic community issues that bear on the health of the people. A primary strategy in their work with the poor and powerless is the promotion of processes that are self-empowering on the part of the people themselves. Such community activity can indeed prove liberating and transforming. It should be noted that palliative measures like those of curative medicine do not fulfill this activating role.

Acceptance of community activist roles in areas of deadly political conflict can leave health workers vulnerable to suspicion by those who interpret community efforts as threatening or subversive. This is precisely what happened in our program between 1980 and 1982, with the death or disappearance of eleven workers in the Department of Chimaltenango and eight in northern Quiché. A painful question has arisen: In training community health workers do we also destine them to death?

"I think that the best way [to heal] a people is to awaken their interest in defending their health in every sense of the word, not only medically.... A first step for the health of our village is to recognize that it is the right, the duty and responsibility of humans as creatures of God to see ourselves as the passing caretakers of this paradise, which today is owned by 15 percent of the people."
— Francisco Currichiche in the film *Seeds of Health* (1976)

Valid answers to this complex question do not come from outside sources, from salon-type or desk-top revolutionaries who propose or endorse strategies from the security and comfort of living rooms or tenured posts. For us here in Chimaltenango, where people have suffered two years of terror, it seems clear that it is for those who daily face these problems and issues, including the possibility of death, to make the decisions that bear on their own destiny and that of their people.

If a health promoter, in the face of terrible tragedy all around — which may have included the loss of family members — makes the decision to continue or reactivate his community efforts in spite of the risks involved, then that worker should be supported. The worker should have access to proper resources as always. To deny a health worker the right and the means to serve his people is irresponsible and immoral, regardless of the jargon to be heard on either side of the political spectrum.

The morality and practicality of training community activists in oppressive societies remains a knotty and heavily complicated question. Suffice it here to say that the line between a worker's role as an agent of change and his or her perhaps inadvertent involvement in political crusading is indeed thin. Ultimately, the worker and the community must make the decisions concerning whether and how to do things — including whether and how to adjust to local realities, particularly when their own survival is at stake.

This is not to say that, for any of us, the goals of power and justice should now become fuzzy or that actions may justifiably become unprincipled. It is not to say that any of us is morally free to abandon the struggle or to seek personal security in some place far removed from it.

A BRIEF POLICY STATEMENT (1983) [Formulated by the board in Guatemala and communicated to program constituencies, supporters, and leaders on both sides of the conflict.]

The Chimaltenango Development Program (Fundación Guatemalteca para el Desarrollo "Carroll Behrhorst") is about to embark on its twenty-second year of work with the people of highland Guatemala. Despite the violence and frustration that have been part of daily life for the past three years, the program continues to pursue its objectives: healing the sick and encouraging processes that bring hope of a better life to the many deprived. But the fact that Guatemala itself now faces an uncertain future raises questions about the status of the program, its ongoing purposes and its relationship to opposing elements on the local political spectrum.

The purpose of this policy statement is to clarify several issues which have caused concern both in Guatemala and among the program's many friends outside Guatemala. Like any human endeavor with people who are submerged in a sea of social, economic and political problems, our work has always been characterized by ambiguities, trials and conflicts. The program staff admit with candor that, together with many successes along the road to health in the highlands, the program has made some false starts, adopted some inappropriate strategies and suffered confusions. Against a backdrop of immense deprivations, it is not easy to keep in motion the wheels of change by which highland people can transform widespread poverty and illness into a more acceptable living environment. When, in addition, a tremendous loss of human and material resources is added to ordinary insecurities, the task becomes vastly more complicated. The recent escalation of political violence in Guatemala not only heightens our awareness of the conflicts attending health and development, but now has the potential of threatening our very survival.

The program has survived to date, even though volunteer health workers have lost their lives to violence in their areas. One major reason for this survival derives from the program's capacity to maintain relationships with the local people by respecting their traditions and their actions in an apolitical, nonaligned manner.

The program enjoys a large reservoir of respect and confidence from all the various groups engaged in the current political struggle, as well as from a majority who remain unengaged. Even the extremes of right and left respect the program because of its constructive activities, which transcend political ideologies. The program takes official sides with no political group in Guatemala.

In responding to requests from leaders of government we have given advice in matters related to health and development, but nothing more. They did not seek and did not get relationship, participation or commitment.

This neutrality has been misunderstood by some and challenged by others, particularly by non-Guatemalans who observe the current crisis from afar. Our answer is that, in the work of health and related development assistance, it is imperative that non-alignment be a part of program policy. We will not succumb to a polarization that might expose the program to reprisal by any side. This policy has the unequivocal support of the local board of directors, whose membership reflects various shades of the Guatemalan political spectrum.

Our political nonalignment does not, of course, allow us to proceed along an ill-defined course without definite purpose or principle. Our commitments are on the side of community stability and of justice for all. The pursuit of these very goals requires some flexibility in taking account of local realities, particularly when the survival of the program and its staff are at stake. No one can respond to fellow humans from beneath six feet of earth in an unnamed burial ground.

Development is an art of the possible, requiring both risk and patience. Our program in Chimaltenango will continue on its determined course.

SOMETHING FROM CHIMALTENANGO (JUNE 13, 1984)

Today is *el día de San Antonio* (the Day of St. Anthony) which, by a centuries-old tradition, should see great dumpings of rain all around. San Antonio is doing his thing. Last night and early today the heavens opened and poured torrents of water inundating the place. Tomorrow, custom also says, the sun will show itself and will do so in increasingly regular turns until el día de Santa Ana, July 28, when downpours will return.

This rain is important not only because it favors the crops and recharges the ground water, but also because people can once again talk and jest about the avalanches and drenches of water that

Picking up and carrying on: A small girl carries ground corn and a baby brother.

befall them all. For a long time feelings and humor have been suppressed. The terrible violence gave low priority to ordinary talk about the rain.

Now work goes on again in all sectors of our program. Long-sought goals are once again being set in view. Objectives can be named and achieved. Dedication to people, and loyalty to those who paid the ultimate price during the violence, make this work both possible and imperative.

A REPORT TO FORMER MEDICAL STUDENTS IN THE CHIMALTENANGO PROGRAM : REFLECTIONS ON RECENT YEARS (MARCH 1986)

I feel like a "prodigal father" embracing his offspring after years of absence. A decade separates many of us. More than 200 medical students, after working in Guatemala, have gone on to successful careers and rewarding practices. During these years an earthquake reduced Chimaltenango to senseless rubble and decimated its people. An innovative health plan based on educating local people as health promoters expanded beyond expectations to produce astonishing results and then was almost destroyed by civil war.

Now at age 63, looking back on these events, I have come to claim the young doctors who worked with me during earlier years as part of my transamerican family. No one who has lived in Guatemala for even a short time can fly home without leaving a part of himself or herself behind. When asked about your time in Guatemala, you no doubt told stories of a lush paradise inhabited by peaceful, self-reliant Mayans. Then, amid all the rumors from 1980 to 1983, you probably wondered how they and we survived the blood baths. I know that a lot of questions have arisen, from news accounts of the earthquake to those of tragic acts of violence to those of the more recent elections. Many details are still too painful for me to easily recall.

After the earthquake of 1976 our work grew rapidly, both in the hospital and in the extension programs. But beginning in 1980 activities were severely curtailed by political violence in the highlands. First, all communication and transportation came to a sudden halt. Guatemala froze as in a dark age. Bus service was stifled in all highland communities, including Tecpán, San Martín, Comalapa, San José Poaquil and Quiché. Chimaltenango stood immobilized. Those few buses that managed to circumvent obstacles were stopped at checkpoints; passengers were made to get off and were searched and sometimes shot on the spot by one political faction or another. Human lives were regarded as expendable. Worse, they were seen as simply insignificant.

The whole world stood aghast, as witnesses to an unbelievable holocaust. Entire towns were annihilated—Las Lomas, Patzac, Xiquin Sanai, begin a long list. Women and children were tortured and killed. The few survivors who managed to escape left behind an empty shell of a village as a memorial to a wretched period marked by barbaric excesses and destruction of human life. Many relocated temporarily to the South Coast or Guatemala City. People from areas up north, such as Huehuetenango and Quiché, were able to seek refuge in Mexico. As a correspondent succinctly put it, "Guatemala has become a nation of widows and orphans."

Many of you have asked specifically about members of the hospital staff. Some died, literally, for what they believed, as martyrs to a cause they had chosen. It was a confusing time —every human soul became a battlefield. We do not judge but only admire the inestimable courage of staff members who pursued their chosen cause to a sacrificial end. It was with the same unconditional fervor that they had thrown their heart and soul into the work of the foundation. Their committed love, humanitarian work and dedication to people will remain forever embedded in the foundation's walls.

The foundation as such has maintained a nonpartisan posture and function, which has granted it some immunity and longevity. We dream that it will eventually become an accepted structure of Guatemala akin to the volcanos, that it will survive civil war, ethnic discrimination, lack of funds and dependence on outside resources both human and material. We could not risk this long-term strategy for the immediate gratification of engaging in politics or of formally choosing sides between political factions—between the tyranny and inhumane excesses of the military and the revolutionary illusion that swift armed violence will deliver Guatemala from its ingrained miseries.

Chimaltenango was hit hardest in 1980-81. After all the other volunteer groups, including the Peace Corps, had pulled out of the area, the foundation board met in 1981 to decide whether to close the hospital or continue. There were no other medical facilities available here at that time. All private programs had closed and public programs were virtually nonexistent. Despite a lower attendance in the hospital, its need was sorely felt. To abandon the people during a time of crisis was unthinkable. A decision was reached to announce *personally* the foundation's nonpartisan stance to the warring parties on both sides, stating our intention to continue functioning on a health and development basis. Meeting with the military in person to convey this information was difficult but essential. We were criticized severely for this by some. Looking back, we consider that these talks were probably the single most important factor in keeping the foundation alive and functioning on its own terms to this day.

It seems inconceivable that any land or people with such a profound spirit and potential, who have every right in the world to prosper, should suffer so much for so long. Our extension program was devastated. Of forty-seven health promoters in the Chimaltenango area, only fifteen remain. ULEU, the land loan program, had been a dream for the future of Guatemalan children—children who suffer one of the world's highest mortality rates. This flourishing program was crippled by the death and displacement of ULEU member-borrowers in the outposts of San Martín, Patzún and San Andrés Itzapa. The manager of ULEU, like many others during that period, was first targeted, then trapped and eliminated by security forces.

Watching this program suffer, with dozens of people losing their lives for what they (and we) believe, was indeed a devastating experience. Participating in its rebirth is like participating in a human miracle. For example, one of our health promoters from San Martín escaped two years ago with only the shirt on his back—his family had been massacred and his village destroyed. He has returned to ask our help in reestablishing a health program for the few survivors in the village. The land loan program is now being reactivated in response to insistent demand, reflecting the indomitable spirit of the Maya and life's longing for itself. I am continually overwhelmed by the insurmountable courage possessed by the people in the face of tragedy — their ability to pick up and begin again.

The hospital census has been rising slowly. It has been a long-cherished dream to see the program become a self-supporting system independent of all foreign help, including my own, and relying totally on native nurses and doctors. That will be a foundation built on national heritage and pride, replacing the debasing image of "white knights" and moving by its own lights and on its own feet into the next century.

Today, as I try placing the last decade in perspective, I sense that what I am writing is not a eulogy but a commencement. The rebuilding of extension programs, health education, nutrition training, family planning, animal and agricultural cultivation, all by Kaqchikel workers rather than by Peace Corps volunteers, amounts to a rebirth on more solid ground. A hospital served by local doctors and a Guatemalan board providing local leadership for the foundation are evidences that the program's chief resources are its own people.

If human life is our most precious possession and death is the highest price that humans can pay, then the people here have paid the price of their continued tenure and future existence in this land a thousandfold. The fact that the foundation has survived the past five years and is being rebuilt by Maya-Kaqchikel people who endured those years means that they have now paid for it. A new foundation will be built on their terms — not mine or yours.

Brother and sister seeing those who came to see them.

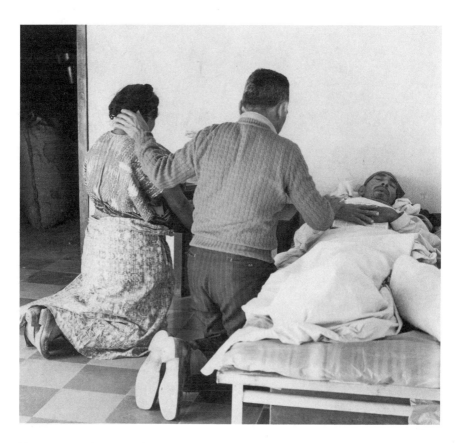

Prayer with a wife and brother-in-law at the Chimaltenango hospital. Who heals? What heals?

8

FOR FUTURE MEDICS

Carroll Behrhorst

FROM AN ADDRESS TO THE AMERICAN MEDICAL
STUDENTS ASSOCIATION (1977)

I will not in this presentation dwell on details of the program that
has evolved in highland Guatemala, but rather will deal with basic
issues in health care as I have come to see them. It should be
remembered that my experience has been largely in communities
of rural Guatemala, so these are issues that have been raised for
me in that context. However, we *do* have thoughts on health
work in what seem more sophisticated communities, like those of
the United States.

Medicine is my calling as it is yours. I do not wish to criticize
the medical profession as bluntly as do some of its current
detractors. But to open our discussion let me present a few
manifest considerations.

- Though morbidity and mortality figures have improved during the past century, the largest achievements have come about through engineering, environmental improvements and some simple immunizations.

- Doctors know how to cure and prevent most ailments around the world, yet they direct their energy and skills to a narrow range of curative work for the near-dead at terrible technological and financial costs. More and more energies and resources are dedicated to extending "sick life" (a phrase of Ivan Illich), generally for the "haves," while even basic care is not available for the "have nots."

- Nature—not the doctor—cures most human ailments, sometimes in spite of the physician, though professionals like to take credit for nature's work. When we give the impression that doctors are responsible for health we are likely to be miserly with information and tools.

- In modern countries, such as the United States, the preponderance of health problems is society related. Excesses in food, drink and smoking are the primary causes of maladies and morbidities in persons over forty; accidents and violence are the most common causes in persons between five and forty. In the poorer parts of the world simple infectious diseases account for most ill health. In the management of these larger groups of human ailments, social and civil communities play important roles.

- The high costs of medical care are well known and few economies can well afford the disproportionately growing costs of doctors and their new technologies. A tendency to focus on who is to pay the bill rather than on how expenditures can be contained and best used compounds this problem.

- Though doctors are still highly rewarded, there is a steady erosion of public trust in the profession, as is evidenced by an increase in malpractice suits—which sometimes causes us to order additional, costly defensive procedures. This problem is a reflection of diminished communication and relevance on the part of many physicians, and it seems foolish to blame lawyers so long as medicine is slow to straighten up its own house.

This list could go on and all its items are underscored in the world's poorer countries.[1] I repeat these familiar judgments to suggest that our medical house is in need of some revamping, including its educational activities. I am convinced that reforms will come about during the next half century, but that these will begin with the next generation—with you.

PATIENTS AS AGENTS

Health has been variously defined and I will not add another definition. Actually, health defies univocal definition since people about the globe have different concepts of health and different ways of describing their health problems. Any definition is likely to be too confining and too inflexible to suggest fully effective responses in actual situations. Health has multiple implications —physical, economic, social, political and cultural—and all these should be taken into account in making fully responsible and humane health provisions. If a monopolistic and perhaps self-serving professional group has in recent decades constricted and

---

[1]In a marginal note Behrhorst cited the summary of a film documentary on the work in Chimaltenango entitled *Seeds of Health*, produced by the World Council of Churches in 1976. The director, Peter Krieg, generalized from learnings in the Guatemalan highlands: (1) The majority of the peoples in rural areas, where most of humankind still live, are hardly reached by modern medical services, especially in "developing" countries. (2) Where people do have access to medical services, these are often expensive and culturally not adapted. (3) Doctors are expensively trained and are thereby motivated to further the isolation, professionalization and specialization of medicine. (4) Medical knowledge and tools, instead of being spread among the people, are increasingly monopolized in the hands of the medical profession. (5) Emphasis in medicine still is more on curing illnesses than on preventing them; many doctors are not able or willing to address the roots of illness which lie outside medicine in social, political or economic areas. (6) The production of drugs and pharmaceutical information are being concentrated in the hands of multinational drug producers whose economic interest lies in selling as many drugs as possible to as many people as possible. (7) Health knowledge and practices belonging to special cultures apart from Western medicine are often pushed into illegality and obscurity; thus, invaluable knowledge, experience and initiatives are lost. (8) Medicine is often approached as an isolated field, rather than as a part of the general physical, psychological, socio-economic and cultural development of humans. (9) In many "developing" countries self-reliance in health is undermined by the introduction of inappropriate medical technologies and medical training, which increases their dependence on aid and technologies from industrialized countries.

dominated the terms of health care, this by no means implies that alternatives are not possible or should not be attempted.

How will new approaches come to pass in this complex life-and-death matter? I wish to suggest that we begin anew with what often seems at the periphery and yet is the most important entity in the health care scheme: the patient, who is the subject and agent of health. Geography, history and culture differ, but the human subject and the human community are always there. I wish to repeat that the doctor of medicine is *not* the custodian of health; people are responsible for their health, as for their responses to life, suffering and death. To a degree, professionals may even have forfeited their claim to be servants of health by neglecting to use that great equalizer, medicine, as a powerful tool to foster individual human responsibility as well as social development and social change.

The route to health in any medical practice would then begin with a dialogue between people and physicians on equal terms, the former articulating felt needs. A period would follow in which the roles on both sides are brought into proper relation and inter-action. Upon establishment of communication, specific objectives would be pursued with a goal of putting knowledge, tools and decision making so far as possible in the hands of the people themselves.

A great deal is being said today about "self-care," but we must recognize that institutional dependencies persist which make this phrase deceptive. Many people have been led to give up their attention to self-experience even when they are well—to say nothing of self-awareness, self-evaluation and self-care when they are ill. This should not detract us from our envisioned goal of putting health care where it properly belongs.

When the mystique and power of the doctor are placed in proper perspective and context, the role of the physician will become once again that of a collaborator and teacher—a true healer enabling people to respond to themselves and their condition.

The physician as teacher.

COMMUNITY INVOLVEMENT

The way forward with many problems of health care, we have said, is to be found by beginning with what has come to seem peripheral. We should not continually fall into the trap of defining our goals in terms of current methods or of defining problems in terms of present solutions — which, in the case of health, have been disease and death oriented. Let us now think, rather, in terms of healthy activities on the part of people, who are meant to be useful, functional and even happy. Accordingly, let us ask: What is the manner in which people go about posing and tackling their health problems?

A common phrase for this is "community involvement," which I define as *the active exercise and celebration of self within the context of community and the common good, for which the basic procedure is communication including problem posing, investigation, decision making, action and evaluation.* I take it as given that people have an inalienable right to make decisions affecting arrangements for their own health in their own communities. If this challenges some current economic, political or professional assumptions, so be it.

My personal experience with community involvement, as we have noted, has been in rural Guatemala where, because of a general lack of big systems and institutions, community organization and engagement may be somewhat simpler than in the United States. Here in the states communities are more varied, fragmented and stratified. They are also more strongly influenced by external institutions, including service and reform organizations, all of which have interests of their own. This can deflect attention from consideration of *local* physical, economic, social and cultural realities. Such special complications in North American settings will have to be faced in a straightforward manner. But the general need and project are similar regardless of geography and culture. Here we might pause to make a simple list of principles and procedures to be affirmed in reclaiming health initiatives for communities.

- Healthy conditions are an integral part of the general goal of justice for all and, like justice, have physical, economic, social, political and cultural dimensions in any actual human setting.

- Expression by individuals and communities of their own health problems and health goals is basic.

- Common reflection on those perceptions by people and health workers together is important, if effectiveness and growth are to occur.

- Sensible planning should follow which includes statements of common goals, problems, priorities and strategies.

- Along with subsequent community action there should be built-in phases of self-evaluation to stay in touch with realities.

Nothing really fundamental will happen for the sake of health in any community until people think together about their situation and its problems. At the same time, they should be aware of possible alternatives that exist along the road to health. Thus, education of a revised sort seems an important preliminary for both the populace and the physician.

First, lay education that increases awareness of individual capacities and responsibilities for self-care and mutual care. Such education will foster a respect for natural processes, for the self and for the community. In actual communities medics could form educational teams with other professionals and community people. These teams, in cooperation with the schools and media, would powerfully communicate personal and community responsibility for health, and set forth the ways of self-healing and mutual healing.

Second, a rededication and restructuring of medical education. More of our medical training will become oriented toward problem solving within a physical and social context, thereby placing the internist with his pills and the surgeon with his knives in proper perspective. A faculty of medicine will see itself as unified in terms of human problem solving, each discipline contributing something toward that function and process. Its graduates will think of teaching and working alongside the farmer, the engineer, the factory worker, the social worker and the minister, to name only a few collaborators.

In communities, both rural and urban, where medical professionals are not available or are unwilling, nurses or local lay healers can be trained for such activities, as well as for symptom recognition and treatment of common health problems. Obviously, the selection, training, scope, supervision and continuing education of such primary health care workers deserve careful attention. They need not, however, be defined as physician assistants or paramedics who labor only in the shadow of a doctor. Their work is not "second class" but "appropriate." Experience has taught us that active involvement in a community organization is itself an effective element of supervision.

Personal and interpersonal care will be only a beginning. Major killers stalk human communities for which the hospital is always too late and the community itself is the first line of defense. This suggests the formation of local health committees or centers. Beginning with local experience, local stories and local fears, the people would move with health workers to make epidemiological inquiries and then plan responsive actions of educational, social and environmental sorts. They would also address that profoundest of all causes of disease—poverty—by identifying and seizing local opportunities for economic development. Such healthy activities should lay claim not only to some of the public responsibilties but also to some of the public funds regularly assigned to health.

PHYSICIANS AS CITIZENS

It may be said, by way of objection, that our special task as doctors is "curing" and that this is more than enough to occupy us. Need we remind ourselves, however, that with the present concentration on curative methods we are not by any means treating all those who need and seek our help, that unserved populations are growing everywhere even as we speak and that we cannot possibly keep up? That our training is much too elaborate, time consuming and costly to prepare a sufficient number of our kind of professionals for all this? Even in the United States we do not at present afford access to all. What about countries to the south where hundreds of thousands must share a single physician or where none is available at all?

I say to professional critics that they should hold their criticisms until they have done one of two things — either have disproved the value of participation by citizens and lay community workers in addressing many actual health problems or have supplied enough doctors who can and will do the job without adding to already astronomic society-wide health costs.

Until then, a part of the answer by necessity will have to be something less sophisticated. I invite you to visit our modest program in the central highlands of Guatemala where traditional medical service is generally not available but where last year sixty responsible Kaqchikel health workers treated more than 30,000 persons who otherwise would not have been served — while at the same time working with community groups on projects for water supply, safety, housing, nutrition, agricultural extension, land acquisition and economic development.

May we look forward to future physicians who will become active leaders of their community in reviewing conditions, programs and policies that bear on the health of all that live there? Is there any profession better qualified than ours to help shape programs and legislation for primary health care and public initiatives for health? By this I do not mean a public concern which raises its head only to lobby for professional interests.

Involvement of the people in making provisions for health will make use of the earth's most creative and most available resource — human beings. It will multiply, both measurably and immeasurably, the quantity and quality of care. Humans, the most sophisticated beings in history, have been bypassed and neglected in approaching public problems of health. As a result, they fail to see themselves as responsible, dignified, violence-free and healing agents. We need not look far to see the massive pathology devolving from this failure.

When the history of medicine is recorded — say around the year 3000 AD — and it is asked what were the great watersheds in medicine, the answer will be found not merely in the discovery of antibiotics or the introduction of aseptic surgery. One of the great transformations will be traced to a time when basic knowledge and initiatives, tools, decision making and organization passed from a short captivity in the hands of the doctor into the hands of the people.

9

THOUGHTS FROM GUATEMALA ON PRIMARY HEALTH CARE

Carroll Behrhorst

LECTURE NOTES, TULANE SCHOOL
OF PUBLIC HEALTH AND TROPICAL MEDICINE   1982-90

"Primary health care" (PHC) is now a world topic. It refers to initiatives needing to be taken literally everywhere in the world. The modern concern began with threats to health in industrialized environments and now extends to conditions bearing on the health of the poorest peoples in the world. We will not here ask the question whether or to what extent the conditions of ill health in both settings have been caused by the very dynamics of modern industrialization and the ideology that tends to go with it.

Public investment in health differs greatly from society to society. In industrialized countries public expenditures on infrastructure and care are, on average, 140 times greater per capita than in Guatemala, to say nothing of the vastly larger difference between private expenditures on both sides, and those differences are widening.

International health conferences in the late 1970s began by making two "reaffirmations": that health is a state of well-being and not merely the absence of disease, and that health is a fundamental human right rather than a privilege. A goal was projected of attaining basic health conditions for all people by the year 2000—such as would permit them to lead socially and economically productive lives or, more generally, to function in ways acceptable to themselves and the community of which they are a part. This was to be achieved through cooperation at many levels. It would include initiatives that take account of vast international inequities. It would also include the understanding that "people have the right and duty to participate individually and collectively in the planning and implementation of their own health care" (World Health Organization 1978).

Such was the Declaration of Alma-Ata in 1978, where primary health care was made a focus of worldwide attention. In 1981 the World Health Assembly, a general organ of the World Health Organization (WHO), adopted a "Global Strategy of Health for All," calling for a social contract between governments and peoples as well as for international cooperation. Since leaders and tools for this kind of health care were not generally available, WHO also convened technical and training consultations (World Health Organization 1979, Mahler 1988).

The experience in highland Guatemala played a role in achieving this international focus. What we wish to do here, however, is not to claim success or influence but to set forth some of the major problems we have encountered, as well as some procedures and guidelines we have adopted in our work with economically pressed communities that are seeking to plan and implement their own health care.

THE WHY OF COMMUNITY PARTICIPATION

Advocates of primary health care point to what a society should do at various levels to assure conditions in which people can be healthy. The Alma-Ata Declaration described this as "essential health care" which, it said, should become "universally accessible to individuals and families in the community through their full cooperation and at a cost that the community and country can afford to maintain at every stage of their development in the spirit of self-reliance and self-determination" (Alma-Ata VI).

Differences begin when people try to specify what goes into those "essential" provisions for which communities and societies bear responsibility. In previous decades public health was identified with engineering works that eradicate environmental causes of disease, but the line between such prevention and some uses of medicine faded with the discovery of bacteria and the growing use of immunization techniques. Today discussion of public efforts includes the control and prevention of communicable infections and health education as well as environmental improvements.

The Alma-Ata Declaration acknowledges that specific community responsibilities would evolve from the local conditions and the special characteristics of the people as they address their own problems of promoting, maintaining and restoring health. It nonetheless tries to make a list of what such primary health care "includes at least": education concerning prevailing health problems and the methods of preventing and controlling them; promotion of food supply and proper nutrition; an adequate supply of safe water and basic sanitation; maternal and child health care, including family planning; immunization against the major infectious diseases; prevention and control of locally endemic diseases; appropriate treatment of common injuries and diseases; and provision of essential drugs (Alma-Ata VII).

Such attempts to state the "basics" raise controversies, as do different descriptions of the proper governmental and professional roles in securing them. Primary health care advocates also point to the important function of nonmedical sectors such as agriculture, animal husbandry, food, industry, education, housing, public works, communications, etc., but they usually shy from pursuing these because this tends to dissolve the distinctive meanings which are important for offices and departments of public health. Reference is simply made to "maximum community participation" and to using a variety of health and community workers as applicable, including traditional practitioners as needed (Alma-Ata VII:5,7).

All this serves to underscore what has been our primary theme: namely, that affected communities are the locus for posing their particular health problems. A two-fold strategy seems required: one which insures, first, that communities actually exercise initiative, inquiry and responsibility in planning and conducting health activities, and one which also insures that relevant information is available to them with respect to resources and available technical possibilities. The process and the problems of gaining community participation and of bringing these two factors together are not set forth in official statements but are what I want to discuss here.

FACING THE PROBLEMS

Elsewhere we have described the potential benefits of community participation. More will be accomplished in this way than can possibly be achieved when measures are merely imposed or are merely therapeutically reactive. Professional approaches to health care simply do not allow for timely and adequate coverage and are more costly. Moreover, participation has intrinsic value for the participants. It offers more possibilities that felt concerns will be taken up. Once in motion, it can be extended to address further community problems and efforts. Thus, community participation may be seen to encourage a local ongoing process of achievement, activities at lower cost, freedom from dependency, and growing conscientization and understanding.

We have also described the nature of participation as the exercise and celebration of the self in a communal process directed toward problem solving. This process was seen to include the steps of problem identification, planning, action and evaluation. The elements of such a process can be further specified to include: the adoption and use of procedures that are accepted as just and equitable by the people; a practice of common reflection as a way of doing things together; the identification of powerful interests inside and outside of the community; the conduct of community assessments based not merely on data gathered by outsiders but on expressions by the people; an analysis of felt problem to their causes; the development of information, precedents, strategies and resources for addressing identified problems; and the performance of adopted programs using impact studies and reviews at decisive points along the way. All these elements will be qualified by local perceptions. Both conditions and beliefs vary from place to place, and any proposed strategy is likely to have not only economic but social, political and cultural implications.

Problems emerge not when we draw up such a list of elements but when we try to go to work on them. At every step along the way the character and vitality of the community are tested. Communities themselves may suffer in some measure from ill-health or malfunction. Their structures are often fragmented. Their priorities are often oriented to specific persons or groups, so that even well-intentioned programs become coopted to enhance the already powerful.

Hence the familiar complaints. There seems a lack of enthusiasm by the people. The same old people dominate the process. Common reflection and intergroup communication are hard to achieve. There is a lack of adequate or genuinely accepted leadership. Goals remain unclear and strategies are not really accepted. Evaluations are flawed and do not really reflect realities. The evaluation indicators are not appropriate.

The reasons generally given for failing to secure participation by the people are apathy, obedience to arbitrary authority, or a reluctance to take risks. None of these is a reason to give up a community health effort. All of these responses—or nonresponses—have causes which can be identified. Indifference may result from a lack of the information needed to make decisions—facts about existing conditions or available tools or about what has been achieved in the past by people in similar situations. Elitist technicians, including doctors, have found it easier or advantageous to withhold information and skills, so that these now seem distant and mystifying; nor have these technicians dealt with the most basic issues of health. Data and information have tended to flow up from the people to the technician, while decision making has flowed down from above. Illiteracy and fragmented communication networks may also thwart the flow of information.

It is because of such deficits that people are not disposed to take risks, even though they see injustice and believe in their community. Moreover, the people will stay that way until they have actually expressed, or even shouted, their own pain together and *want* a problem to be solved. This is the first inescapable step toward community participation. The second preliminary step is equally necessary: they must see an objective as within their reach, which means seeing some ways and means, before they will take bold steps together.

For all these reasons, a strategy is required for the very problem of achieving community participation. This strategy may need to be used again and again when a community is impressed by obstacles and is in danger of slipping back into apathy. Central to this strategy (here we borrow some terms that are now being used by similar communities elsewhere in the world) is the work of "animators" who elicit "generative themes" and present "codes" (Hope and Timmel 1984).

Trained animators are persons who clearly and acceptably share the local identity and who have also acquired an open attitude. These persons deliberately engage community people in conversation on casual occasions and in comparatively unstructured meetings, perhaps in times of crisis. They are trained to listen. What are the people really thinking? What concerns, fears, deprivations and aspirations do the people express? What are the traditions, values and patterns that shape what they say? What achievements do they recall from the past? Why were these important? How did they come about? What do they see as their strengths and whom do they see as their leaders?

Emerging from such conversations are generative themes or clusters of issues about which the people do have strong feelings and which gain responses from person to person. Since these themes are emotionally charged, they bring forth both thought and passion. Once they are brought out into the open, people begin to doubt their doubts and to look at their problems again.

Health worker gets a second opinion.

By way of taking up these themes together, the animator then forms and presents what may be called codes. These are concrete "insider" presentations of the expressed concerns of the people by means of pictures, cartoons, stories, diagrams, masks or plays. Such presentations cause excitement, humor, hilarity, commonality and energy. Energies so aroused may then be channelled toward actually posing a problem together, inspecting that problem for its causes and breaking down larger problems into a sequence of smaller ones for solution. In the course of this procedure, leadership can emerge. The community initiatives re-quired for primary health care can begin anew.

We have not here treated the serious external obstacles which may be encountered along the way. "Expert" visitors can some-times subvert a community process. The people remain uncon-vinced or lose heart if program proposals are presented as "community oriented" even when they are not actually community based, if the people are "allowed to participate" but not to do it themselves.

There may also be instability or undependability in the basic infrastructure, agencies or programs of the larger society that are supposed to support community efforts. For lack of a larger poli-tical will and agreement on PHC goals, community initiatives may even appear threatening and bring down professional or official reaction, even brutal military reaction (Heggenhougen 1984). Such violence is bad for the people's health and also bad for the people's programs in support of their own health. Continuing to work with the community in the face of powerful outside forces might seem one of the highest expressions of human health, but in many places today this is not the kind of health activity that increases life expectancy.

We are a long way from achieving the supportive and stable policies at national and international levels that are called for by international advocates for primary health care. There is no more important health provision for the future than the establishment of peace accords with justice—where justice is seen to include "the right and duty to participate individually and collectively in the planning and implementation of health care" (Alma-Ata IV).

GUIDELINES FOR PRIMARY HEALTH CARE
FROM THE GUATEMALAN EXPERIENCE

Following is a summary of ground-level practices and findings that have grown up in the course of our cooperation with rural villages to improve, at one and the same time, both community participation and community provisions for health.

- Primary health work begins in dialogue with the people whose health is at issue. They raise the concerns. People everywhere have their own ideas about what should be done with their lives, health and homes. The effective health worker listens, treats people as equals in decision making and does not force ideas and standards on those served.

- Health has many facets—economic, social, political and cultural—which differ from community to community. Any of these may surface when the epidemiology of a human health problem is being considered. It is less than adequate to depend on outreach programs and service schemes if their guiding policy is not an empowering process, and this means making use of physical, economic, social, political and cultural capacities in addressing problems.

- Proper care of any ailment requires treatment of causes, not merely amelioration of pain. A public health program aimed exclusively at curing the sick will have little effect on the health of the rural poor. A program that includes preventive medicine, nutrition and hygiene will fare somewhat better, but it too will fail to do the job. A program expanded by family planning and increasing crop yields on the family plot will accomplish more. However, a program that fails to deal with the fundamental problem—ownership of land or acquisition of some stakes—will achieve no more than a modest and precarious success.

- The truly successful public health program among the rural poor will tackle problems of both economic and political development. This by no means suggests that program leaders should plunge into controversial national issues or ally themselves with specific political movements. They may, in fact, be required to stand aside from factional politics—if they are to stand with people who are still without broader political power. Yet there are levels below those of

national politics where the people can learn to control their own lives
through economic and political activity. A cooperative is a good
example, since it both responds to economic need and builds local
leadership. The cooperative is no panacea, but it is often a practical
move in the right direction, laying a foundation for people to gain
power in the economics and politics of survival.

- "Health" is perceived differently in different societies. Rural societies,
  both by circumstance and by choice, have usually depended on
  natural processes and nontechnical interventions to maintain or restore
  health. Industrialized societies, by contrast, have viewed health
  within the context of administered procedures, application of
  technology and chemically-produced remedies. Whereas rural peoples
  have stressed dependence on "spirit" and on balanced relationships
  with fellow human beings and with nature, modern medicine has
  largely abstracted from these relations to concentrate on causes and
  techniques amenable to strict application and measurement. When
  working with the rural poor, one should always be sensitive to their
  traditions and their felt needs.

- The concept of "development" should be reexamined. Great
  allotments of time, paper, food and jet fuel have been expended in
  development efforts, often with little lasting effect. Clean water and
  malaria control may help diminish disease but do not in themselves
  furnish the tools and procedures for building a health promoting
  society. Genuine development requires creative processes that
  encourage both self-reliance and a sharing of available resources. The
  point is to seek measures that create and activate a community, rather
  than leave it passive and waiting.

- A program that relies too heavily on outside technical and financial
  assistance is destined for trouble. Almost any technically trained
  person, regardless of nationality, is considered an outsider in areas
  inhabited by the rural poor. There is an enormous difference in
  outlook between the urbanized technician and the rural poor. The
  technician is usually assured of a physically comfortable existence,
  while the poor person struggles to survive from day to day. This
  discrepancy alone accounts for radical differences of perception. Poor
  persons are not fools and must be thoroughly convinced that the
  technocrat's arguments and procedures are valid for them before they

will risk deviation from age-tested patterns of living, especially if they have to pay for them now or in the future.

- Beware the cry for "higher standards." Professionals are disposed to boost standards, thereby increasing the need for equipment and expertise and driving up costs beyond the reach of a humble community by itself. Quality should never be equated with high cost.

- Local community health committees should be organized and functioning before the first aspirin or dressing is handed out. These committees will then select the people to be trained, supervise them and discipline them. They will also help set the standards of service and the prices to be charged.

- The outside help needed in terms of materials, labor, direction, training and supervision should conform to local customs and traditions. A visiting physician, technician or trainer will prepare local counterparts as quickly as possible.

- Training programs should permit community workers to continue their usual work and maintain their family and community relationships, keeping absences from home to a minimum. Long absences in a different setting can make a return to the community difficult and sometimes impossible.

- Curative training requires the use of clinical teaching with actual patients in a dispensary or hospital. When workers are on the job, frequent consultation is essential, though arrangements will depend on local circumstances. The treatment of ailments should be in accordance with symptoms and should not attempt diagnoses, which are prone to error even by people with sophisticated schooling. Our experience is that symptom treatment results in relatively low error. Trainees must be clear on what not to treat as well as about what to treat and how. The future of nonprofessional curing depends on this.

- Ideally, program income should cover all ordinary expenses. Dependence on outside finances saps local responsibility and may place the supply of services and materials in jeopardy.

- Progress takes time. Programs formulated by technicians seeking quick, measurable results seldom live up to expectations. Genuine change requires commitment and patience.

References

Heggenhougen, H. Kris
    1984 Will Primary Health Care Efforts be Allowed to Succeed? Social Science and Medicine 19(3):217-24.
Hope, Anne and Sally Timmel
    1984 Training for Transformation: A Handbook for Community Workers. Vol. 1. Gweru, Zimbabwe: Mambo Press.
Mahler, Halfdan
    1988 Social Justice—The Underpinning for Health Leadership Development. Ira Hiscock Public Lecture at the University of Hawaii School of Public Health. In: The Congressional Record—Senate 1988(Oct.17):S16404-7.
World Health Organization
    1978 Alma-Ata Declaration on Primary Health Care.
    1979 Formulating Strategies for Health for All by the Year 2000.
    1981 Global Strategy for Health for All by the Year 2000.
    These are nos. 1-3 in: Health for All series. Geneva: WHO Office of Publications.

LEARNINGS
FOR HEALTH CARE
AROUND THE WORLD

A hundred times every day I see the great pride, dignity and humility of the local Maya. If we tarnish their dignity and respect for themselves, then we have failed regardless of how many privies we have built, how many names we have put on the rolls, or how many bodies we have rescued from disease. If we cannot maintain absolutely the dignity of the native people, then better that we go back to Kansas or New York or wherever we come from.... Racial pride, dignity, identity, integrity, these are the things that will determine the future of humans, including their health, whether in Chimaltenango, Saigon, Harlem or Wichita.

— Carroll Behrhorst
*Thoughts on Community Services in Low-Production,
Physically Deprived Nations (1973)*

Open heart surgery is medicine (they say)—treating tuber-
culosis by a fight against poverty and malnutrition and
inequitable land tenure and social injustice is not. Neonatal
laboratories are medicine—nutrition for expectant mothers is
not. I say bull....

There need be no humans in any community or city block or
civil unit on the planet who cannot properly serve themselves
or be served by someone from that same community, regardless
of economic status or location.

> — *Alternatives in Community Health Care: Some Notes*
> *(For a consultation in Cuernavaca, Mexico, 1973)*

Most doctors of medicine demand that patients come to
"their" places, "their" clinics, "their" hospitals, "their"
institutions for service. Examination of the situation,
however, shows us that health problems do not have their
origin in the doctors places (except in the instance of
iatrogenic diseases!) but rather have their roots "out there" in
the homes and in the communities. That being the case, the
knowledge and skills of the physician should be taken to
people "out there".

> — *Lecture on receiving the E. H. Christopherson*
> *Award of the American Academy of Pediatrics (1988)*

10

THE "AHK'OHN UTZ" OF CHIMALTENANGO
The Medical Value of Cultural Understanding

Michael H. Logan

A wind arose early that day. Hopes were rising and the villagers of San Miguel Kotsea knew that the seasonal rains would soon arrive. Don Manuel Otzoy had long awaited the closing of the dry season. So too had his two eldest sons. Soon they and their father would plant *milpa*, a small, sloping plot of land given annually, as it had been for centuries, to maize and black beans. The Otzoy family, as so many others near and far, were eager to meet once again the challenge of living. Their milpa was indeed their life. As it fared, so too would they.

For Manuel, that morning of wind and darkening clouds was different from seasons past. While his sons would begin to work the land, Manuel, at least this day, would not. Leticia, his three-year-old daughter, was gravely ill. By mid-morning Manuel had carried Leticia from Kotsea to El Tablón, where they waited for the bus. It finally arrived. Two hours later they reached Chimaltenango. Stepping from the bus onto the plaza street, Manuel whispered to Leticia, "This is where the doctor lives."

Leticia entered the clinic in the arms of her father. She vaguely recalled that her mother remained at home in Kotsea. Doña Matilda was busy making the midday meal for her sons, who would soon return from the family milpa. Leticia and Manuel, however, waited in the courtyard of the clinic. Leticia had not really heard when her father had said, "This is where the doctor lives." Manuel was painfully aware, though, of the ordeal at hand.

They waited. A nurse later approached them and Leticia was taken to an examining room. A physician then entered and the door was quietly shut. Manuel passed among others in the courtyard. He noticed many things he would normally have overlooked. The laundry drying on a hibiscus hedge. The sounds of women in the rear of the courtyard patting out tortillas for their kin who had been hospitalized.

Children ran about, their antics and yells being occasionally overcome by the traffic noise of Chimaltenango's busy plaza. «¡Guate! ¡Guate!» — another bus was soon to leave Chimaltenango for the capital. In the courtyard Manuel looked skyward. Clouds were building. Soon the rains would come.

Someone called Manuel's name; he rose and was taken into a room. There he learned, in the gentle and reassuring words of the doctor, that Leticia was indeed gravely ill. Examination had established the presence of acute enteritis, otitis media and severe bronchial inflammation. Other problems were spelled out. There was anemia and malnutrition. An improved dietary regimen was detailed, along with the requirement of providing boiled drinking water once they returned to Kotsea. Leticia would have to be hospitalized, though, for two days at minimum. Manuel seemingly understood and agreed to all that was conveyed. He also knew that medicines and vitamins would be administered here. More should be taken once they were home in Kotsea. This was Leticia's third trip to Chimaltenango.

On the patient roster that morning were the names of other children: Benjamín, Sergio, Claudia, Ramón, María Teresa. The diagnosed problems were all too similar to those drawing the strength and vitality from Leticia: upper respiratory infection,

Waiting to see the good healer in the hospital yard.

gastroenteritis, acute dehydration, anemia. And in more cases than not, there was physical wasting due to malnutrition.

Of the five children seen that morning when Leticia was hospitalized, two never returned to the clinic during the season of rains. They fell into the alarming reality of Guatemala's health statistics: approximately 80 percent of rural children are malnourished (GHRSP 1988); in some villages 100 percent of the children test positive for helminthic parasitization (Scrimshaw and Tejada 1970); nearly 50 percent of Indian newborns will never reach the age of five (Early 1982, Hearst 1985). Sergio and María Teresa were among those lost that summer. Leticia's luck was better. She was living. The milpa was now growing in Kotsea.

Many other problems faced the people seen by the doctor, Carroll Behrhorst, in Chimaltenango. Not enough land, never enough milpa. Families broken as men left the highlands to gain seasonal work on the plantations along the south coast. Rural families migrating into the cities, families woefully ill-equipped to survive. City children in gangs. Children addicted to glue sniffing (Zinner 1990). And everywhere there was violence (Carmack 1988, Layton 1981, Peterson 1987). People would simply disappear, some to be found days or weeks later in a gulley filled with trash. Entire villages had been targeted for liquidation (Clay 1983, Falla 1983). The aftermath of violence is not only seen daily, it is also seen everywhere. At times the scenes are unfathomable—a boy witnessing his father being beaten to death, then crucified and castrated (Sexton 1985:368).

Turmoil, poverty, hunger, prejudice—these are the stark realities of Guatemala, the "Land of Eternal Spring." The outcome of their interaction is a deadly force that both underlies and perpetuates the glaring health needs of Guatemala's indigenous peoples. These realities of life were reflected clearly in the weathered face and soiled clothing of Don Manuel Otzoy. Their presence was equally clear in the frail body of Leticia.

DISEASE, HEALING AND CULTURE

For the peoples of San Miguel Kotsea, there are two primary divisions of sickness: *yabilh chakular*, "malevolent sickness," and *yabilh utzilag*, "simple sickness" (see Foster 1976). Symptoms of Leticia's illness, while important for describing it to the doctor, were of less concern to her father than the ultimate cause of her sliding strength and suffering. He, like all members of the Otzoy family, needed to know why she was sick. Was it the black beans she had eaten, along with the pinch of brown sugar that she so much enjoyed, that caused the excessive heat within her body? If so, then cooling teas and green vegetables should soon help restore her lost, though essential, equilibrium (see Logan 1977). If this were Leticia's problem, then it was yabilh utzilag. Here there was still cause for much concern, but less than in cases of yabilh chakular. Behrhorst knew this.

He also knew of sickness owing to factors other than the natural forces of heat and cold. He had treated children, after all, who were victims of "soul-loss," *yabilh quixiqui* (see Logan 1979, 1987, Rubel et al 1984). As Manuel and his fellow villagers had carefully explained to Doc, the blood of such victims, many of whom had later died, changes color from the healthy states of black and red. It changes from *uk kik* and *k'iuk kik*, to an unhealthy white, *suk kik*, then to the most dangerous of all—*k'an kik*, yellow blood.

Behrhorst had learned, as well, of the machinations of *ahkitz* (sorcerers), who could visit many harms on those who broke from *costumbre*, the traditional Mayan way of life. What may seem to have been a chance encounter with a rabid dog was anything but that. It was by design. The person involved may not fall immediately ill, but in time this frightening event may finally force the soul from the victim's body. If the resulting sickness progressed and therapy made no headway against the patient's suffering, then it was yabilh chakular, malevolent sickness. Doc knew this. He was aware of El Cadejo, a malevolent dog of the night, one that could be controlled by an ahkitz. El Cadejo fed on the vomit of drunks and was always a potential presence in the moonlit landscape. Villagers of Kotsea also knew of other spirit beings. So, too, did Doc.

La Llorona was one. Another was El Sombredudo. At night, along creeks and especially near the village *pila* (public water spigot), La Llorona had been sighted. Her pale skin and flowing white gown, her light hair and golden jewelry, made her over-whelmingly attractive to wayward, intoxicated men. Her counter-part was equally alluring to unsuspecting young women. With his large moustache and larger straw hat, El Sombredudo would always wait for the unsuspecting daughters of the village who chose to break from normative tradition. Each of these nightly agents was beautiful and appealing. Yet each was an antithesis of their illusion. They were hideous, fetid beings. As with El Cadejo, they could capture one's soul.

Deep within the mountains encircling San Miguel Kotsea reside *los naguales*, the animal companion spirits that join each and every person as they enter into life (see La Farge and Byers 1931, Saler 1967). Some infants are strong and grow quickly. One reason for their good fortune is that they had been matched, by fate alone, with powerful naguales. From within the mountains a force favors certain children, but not all. Companion animals, like people, differ; all are not equal. The naguales linked to Sergio and María Teresa were frail and sickly. These children of Patzún, who died some weeks after returning from Chimaltenango, never had much chance of living. Their fate had been sealed as a result of weak and decaying naguales. Doc knew the physical reasons why they had perished, but he also understood that little good would come from criticizing a people's belief in animal companion spirits. There were immediate physical problems to address: not enough land, malnutrition, bacteria-laden water and poor public hygiene.

Shortly after he had seen Leticia and Manuel, Doc was called to a Kaqchikel home in Chetol. Upon entering the dirt-floored, single room structure, he waited a few seconds for his eyes to adjust to the dim light. In a corner he found a young boy lying deadly still on his *petate*, a sleeping mat made of woven reeds. The boy had been placed a few feet from the three-stone cooking hearth. There it was warm. Tortillas from the morning meal remained on the griddle. In the ashes below were two small ceramic pots of black beans. Rays of sunlight cut through the gray haze of smoke that filled the room. The aroma of wooden embers and cooked corn remained. It was a smell Doc encountered daily during his many years in the highlands, and one he had come to love. He had also encountered, and all too frequently, sights identical to what he was witnessing, a motionless child lying on a small mat, staring blankly into the dim light. This boy did not blink, although dozens of black gnats had been trapped on the drying surface of his half-open eyes. Doc rose and quietly spoke with the parents. Their son would need to go to Chimaltenango — at once.

During their drive from Chetol they explained to Doc that two days ago a local curandero had come to their home to perform *una limpia*, a cleansing ritual, to remove the sickness from their ailing son, Benjamín. Benjamín's body had been swept with fragrant herbs. A raw egg had been passed over his body in the pattern of the cross. Copal incense was burned. A tea made of *pericón (Tagetes lucida)* was administered. All that could be done was done, yet their son only grew worse. Yabilh chakular, the parents thought.

Luckily, however, they remembered that an older cousin of their son was leaving the next morning for the capital and one of the interim stops for the bus would be Chimaltenango. He was instructed to carry word to the *ahk'ohn utz*, the healer who lives there. The following afternoon was when Doc drove to Chetol and was led to the house where the boy lay on the petate. An hour later Doc's jeep pulled back into Chimaltenango's plaza and then quickly stopped at the front doors of his clinic. Soon they were inside, and Benjamín was placed on intravenous therapy. Doc explained that it was indeed yabilh chakular, yet he had medicine that would help. This was his way of giving "una limpia."

The doctor from Chimaltenango was never outwardly critical of the medical beliefs and practices of the Mayan peoples (see Orellana 1987). After all, he had been in Guatemala for only a few short decades and they for millennia. He would constantly remind other gringos who had recently arrived to work at his clinic that the Mayans were "the ones who know" (*los que saben*). They were also the ones that most needed help.

I first met Doc — where else? — in Chimaltenango. From that day on my life changed as a person, an educator and an anthropologist. From his lessons I have been able to reach thousands of

Basket in the Chimaltenango market: An egg for a healing ritual.
An egg a day (plus peppers) for health.

students about the real meaning of human maladies like marasmus and kwashiorkor. These are not merely abstract concepts from a textbook in pathology. They are the Benjamíns of the world who, at age three, have yet to walk because they are so malnourished. Behind the sobering statistics I convey in a lecture about mortality in peasant societies there will always be Sergio and María Teresa. They were among the 50 percent that never reach the age of five. And in my talks to students there is always Doc. They learn why, through his marvelous insight and skill, Leticia Otzoy was brought to Chimaltenango, and why she and now her own children enjoy a "new dawn."

The rains have come again to San Miguel Kotsea. The Land of Eternal Spring is green again. There is a rising hope in Guatemala which was captured in the words that Manuel spoke to Leticia as he stepped from the bus onto the plaza of Chimaltenango. "This is where the doctor lives." And so he does. *Nuevo amanecer, Ahk'ohn Utz.*

References

Carmack, Robert M.
    1988 The Mayan Indians and the Guatemalan Crisis. Norman: University of Oklahoma Press.
Clay, Jason (ed.)
    1983 Voices of the Survivors: The Massacre at Finca San Francisco, Guatemala. Cultural Survival 10:1-106.
Early, John D.
    1982 Structure and Evolution of a Peasant System: The Guatemalan Population. Boca Raton: University Presses of Florida.
Falla, Ricardo
    1983 The Massacre at the Rural Estate of San Francisco — July, 1982. Cultural Survival 7(1):43-45.
Foster, George M.
    1976 Disease Etiologies in Non-Western Medical Systems. American Anthropologist 78:773-782.
GHRSP
    1988 Guatemala Health Rights Support Project Report. Washington, D.C., 1747 Connecticut Ave., N.W.

Hearst, Norman
  1985 Infant Mortality in Guatemala: An Epidemiological Perspective.
        International Journal of Epidemiology 14:575-581.
La Farge, Oliver and Douglas Byers
  1931 The Year Bearer's People. Middle American Research Series
        Publication No. 3. New Orleans: Tulane University.
Layton, Kelly
  1981 Chimaltenango: A State of Siege. Anthropology Resource Center
        Newsletter 5(2):4.
Logan, Michael H.
  1977 Anthropological Research on the Hot-Cold Theory of Disease:
        Some Methodological Suggestions. Medical Anthropology 1:87-
        112.
  1979 Susto Causality Among the Cakchiquel of Guatemala. Culture,
        Medicine and Psychiatry 3:153-166.
  1987 New Perspectives on an Old Disorder: Fright-Sickness in
        Oaxaca. Reviews In Anthropology 14:167-181.
Orellana, Sandra L.
  1987 Indian Medicine in Highland Guatemala: The Pre-Hispanic and
        Colonial Periods. Albuquerque: University of New Mexico
        Press.
Peterson, Robert L.
  1987 The Urban-Rural Confrontation in Guatemala: Political Violence,
        Cultural Deteriorization, and Economic Decline. SECOLAS
        Annals 28:47-59.
Rubel, Arthur J., Carl O'Nell, and Rolando Collado-Ardon
  1984 Susto: A Folk Illness. Berkeley: University of California Press.
Saler, Benson
  1967 Nagual, Witch, and Sorcerer in a Quiché Village. In: Magic,
        Witchcraft, and Curing. J. Middleton, ed. pp. 69-100. Garden
        City, New York: The Natural History Press.
Scrimshaw, Nevin S. and C. Tejada
  1970 Pathology of Living Indians as Seen in Guatemala. In:
        Handbook of Middle American Indians, No. 9. T.D. Stewart,
        ed. pp. 203-225. Austin: University of Texas Press.
Sexton, James D. (trans. and ed.)
  1985 Campesino: The Diary of a Guatemalan Indian. Tucson:
        University of Arizona Press.
Zinner, John
  1990 In Guatemala, No One Is Safe...Not Even the Children. New
        York Times, Oct. 27, p. 23(L).

11

JOINING COMMUNITY STRUGGLES FOR HEALTH
Anthropological Notes on Learning from "The Other"

H. Kris Heggenhougen

Some years ago, while working as an anthropologist at the London School of Hygiene and Tropical Medicine, I was confronted with the remark: "Anthropology is jolly interesting, so long as it doesn't get in the way of 'the real stuff'!" For many working in international public health "the real stuff" was biomedicine and rigorous epidemiology grounded in biostatistics—the "real" or "hard" sciences.

I found the comment disturbing since I worked in an interdisciplinary center which fostered a collegial interrelationship between the social and biomedical disciplines as a fruitful approach to understanding public health problems, especially in cross-cultural settings. Its philosophy was similar to that expressed by V. Ramalingaswami (1986) in an article entitled "The Art of the Possible": Progress in the field of international public health will not depend simply on new discoveries in either the biomedical or the social sciences but rather on a creative joining of current knowledge and practices from both sides of the spectrum.

Here in the Harvard Medical School and the Harvard School of Public Health (as increasingly in the London School) anthropology is making its presence felt and its relevance recognized. Changes have occurred since the 1950s when Benjamin Paul (1955), a father of medical anthropology, made important contributions to Guatemalan studies while in the Harvard School of Public Health but was never granted tenure. Medical anthropology is now, in fact, a central discipline of the Department of Social Medicine at Harvard. The current receptivity affords an opportunity and a challenge for anthropologists to join with workers in other disciplines, on equal footing and without subservience to biomedical taskmasters, in making contributions to improving public health that are as much the "real stuff" as anything else.

Outside the academy we have witnessed a growing acceptance of sociocultural factors as relevant for community health programs. Most countries now speak of "primary health care" and are establishing corresponding public policies. The World Health Organization defines health in terms of "physical, mental and social well-being and not merely the absence of disease." Popular books have appeared by scientists bearing such titles as *The Tao of Physics* and *The Turning Point* (Capra 1976, 1982), along with influential articles in scientific journals like George Engel's "The Need for a New Biomedical Model" (1977). We have seen a shift in therapeutic terminology from phrases suggesting a "magic bullet" to phrases describing a "web of causality." To those for whom the ultimate bedrock of pathogenicity still lies in hard-nosed biomedicine and tightly drawn quantitative epidemiology and for whom anything else is at best "jolly interesting," Marilyn Nations (1986) poses a question: Is this "quantitative rigor" or "rigor mortis"?

This change is ascribable, most of all, to practical exemplars. Carroll Behrhorst was one who, first in practice and later in teaching, redirected international public health efforts to embrace more encompassing parameters. One of the legacies of his work in highland Guatemala is the now recognized necessity to look beyond traditional biomedical boundaries. Biomedicine and curative services are, of course, extremely important for the thousands of Kaqchikel who suffer life-threatening maladies. We need only think of the many agonizing parents struggling to save the lives of their children from a medicable disease. However, much more is required to reduce the disproportionately high morbidity and mortality rates of the Guatemalan Maya and of many other societies similarly ensnared in poverty throughout the world.

That is what Behrhorst learned through practical experience during his early days in Chimaltenango and it is the lesson he conveyed to those who came to know him as patients, colleagues, students or friends. I am among those who learned this with him and who, like him, learned it by living among the Kaqchikel. The interconnectedness of multiple causes came home to me by dwelling with those affected. The impossibility — even destructiveness — of staying within a medicalized focus and ignoring local perceptions and multiple causes including land hunger, migrant labor and indebtedness became an unforgettable lesson.

It was while living within the local world of the village of Simajuleu in the early 1970s that I learned what it means to become an anthropologist and gained convictions about what to convey to future generations of students considering this field. The ideas were not new; they were centuries old. They combined words and melody of a primordial ecological song which can, however, become drowned in the (sometimes missionary) thunder of one-sided convictions about the "correct way" and the "real stuff." It is a song in need of repeated revival and Behrhorst was a revivalist.

Since this song includes both a theme and variations, learning it entailed for me a number of specific though interrelated lessons. These included a dawning recognition of the importance of context, of learning different ways of learning, of understanding "the other," and of posing questions as well as answers including the question "so what?"

Clean water flows from a new pila in Simajuleu.

CONTEXT—"IT ALL DEPENDS"

Anthropologists repeatedly say, "Well, it all depends." This does not imply that we are complete relativists who do not believe in even a minimal set of universal human moral or ethical standards. Of course we do. The holocaust remains the holocaust. It is possible to affirm the importance of preserving cultural diversity while at the same time—and partly for this very reason—unequivocally rejecting torture, cultural imperialism or genocide. Groups such as Cultural Survival, Inc. (Cambridge, Massachusetts) and the International Working Group for Indigenous Affairs (Copenhagen) are seeking to clarify moral codes needed to guide inter-relationships between culturally diverse groups of people—precisely because we not only recognize but also value diversity.

However, anthropologists generally shy from talking in absolutes. We are interested in the specific and in differences —thus complementing epidemiologists who look for universals and overall patterns. We constantly introduce examples of how culture and health are interrelated, and maintain that cultural characteristics are reflected in specific epidemiological patterns (Dunn and Janes 1986). We do not, however, want to be boxed in by "culture" in some limited sense of that word (Kaufert 1990). People are not tin soldiers uniformly marching to the tune of a social code. It is important to give attention to the total context including the physical and biological environment, social forms and social status, tools and ways of working, economic and power relationships, cultural memories and observances, all of which help to shape the way people live their everyday lives in their local worlds. Consideration must also extend to wider forces impinging upon local communities.

Studying the interrelated aspects of human contexts differs in noteworthy ways from the study (for example) of the life cycle of the schistosome. In the study of humans we use more explicit qualitative considerations along with quantitative and descripive methods. This, of course, raises questions concerning the assumption of a value-free science. In what sense and to what extent is this the case? When Behrhorst came to recognize the importance of context for the health of the people he could not remain dispassionate or neutral. No more could we when we came to live and work with the villagers.

Anthropologists who claim objective neutrality in their study of peoples and communities would do well to reflect on their own history. One aspect of that history is the service rendered by this profession to colonial administrators. Anthropological insights have been used to better understand, and so more firmly to administer, the lives of colonized peoples. This venal heritage remains despite interventions on the part of some anthropological workers to abate the cultural imperialism of impinging powers.

Today, in the area of international aid or public health, anthropologists are again asked to work, in some degree, as handmaidens. We are asked to find the cultural buttons which can be pushed to make the "target" people cooperate—this time, presumably, for their own health and welfare. Such a use of anthropological findings, insofar as it may disregard the perspectives, goals and self-determination of the people themselves, seems scarcely less a manipulation than that which took place 50 and more years ago. It defeats the practice of the "art of the possible" in that it does not genuinely join two disciplines in a real setting, but rather employs one as subservient to the "scientifically correct" interventions of the other.

Another historical root of the anthropological enterprise lies in a desire to achieve critical distance from one's own society, to find or compare alternatives. Such anthropological study allows us to inspect our own values and cultural characteristics in juxtaposition with those of others—to recognize that there is a difference. It affords a two-way gaze for better understanding both ourselves and others, and for engagement with those others without presuming that our own values are always to be used as the norms.

Even in this approach, however, some caution is indicated. A wonderful "On The Far Side" cartoon bears the caption "Anthropologists! Anthropologists!" (warning of their coming) and depicts "the natives" hiding away their television sets, VCRs and other electronic equipment as the scholars, pit-helmets and all, step out of their canoes and approach the huts. The point is clear. Disparate groups of people are often quite accurately aware of how others want to see them and sometimes try to conform to that image. It is easier for them that way—at least in the short-run.

James Thurber quipped that "a critic is a person who looks in the microscope and discovers his own eye." This contains a warning not only for anthropologists but also for people in the "hard" sciences. Interests have a bearing on the very choice of what is studied, on the funding of one set of research questions rather than another, and on how research is conducted. Such choices are inescapably value laden. It is best to acknowledge this. How are priorities being set and by whom? In going to work in a cultural setting different from our own, we can plainly ask whose values are operative—ours, theirs or both? These questions took on flesh and blood for me in Simajuleu.

THE IMPORTANCE OF BEING THERE—
LEARNING DIFFERENT WAYS OF LEARNING

Experiences in highland Guatemala impressed me with the importance of gaining firsthand experience and, so far as possible, an insider's insight into the lives of people with whom one wishes to cooperate. It was day-to-day experiences that had changed Behrhorst's early perceptions of how best to practice medicine in Chimaltenango—he described this as a "conversion" and as "a missioner being missionized." It was such experiences that brought me, a student and would-be anthropologist, to a next lesson: namely, that there is more than one way of learning.

In my village hut in Simajuleu (which means literally, "the edge of the world") I reflected on the importance of "being there." To give a flavor of the different kind of "learning" which this implies, let me repeat something I have transcribed from field notes made two decades ago (see Heggenhougen 1992).

> I was at the "edge of the world," then, to understand and make sense of the totality of this new reality. Francisco, Ernesto, Inez, and Nana... a whole group of unknown people. The fields. The sheep and the pigs. The handshakes. The eating and talking. The working, walking and incessant *mandados* (errands). The greetings, which seemed at first repetitive. This culture in its

entirety was my discrete anthropological subject. My challenge was to compre-hend this culture in order properly to evaluate a health program in this context.

By being there I was in the process of becoming an anthropologist (I hesitate in writing this term).... Why could not one do this in the classroom and the library? What, at bottom, was so important about fieldwork? Was this, along with other reasons that could be given, also a rite of passage? If so, in addition to the observations, analysis and recording, what was supposed to happen?

And that was it. Exactly this was supposed to happen. Later I would review it with my head also; for now the important thing was what was happening. The anthropologist's feeling must lead his thoughts into the experience, if he is actually to encounter and then to apprehend "the other." What a realization for a staid Norwegian: head and heart!

What fieldwork was really all about was being touched by a different reality. That is what I had to "learn." It included what happened to me as much as anything else—not just what I read and saw and understood but what I ate, smelled and felt. What I experienced.

The pigs waking me at three, four, five in the morning...the hundred pounds of wheat on my back...the kuxa...the mud...the wind, the hailstorm and being soaked to the bone...the smoke in my eyes while eating beans with my fingers, the tortillas...the charcoal dust and no water to wash or drink. Esteban playing his cracked guitar, smiling with eyes that had been blind three years, suddenly crying "Why? Why?" The marriages, wakes and funerals, the malnutrition, amputation of a finger... the pride, the humility, the persistence, the weakness. Tata's laugh and rotting teeth, his patched clothes and his thin body walking every day stooped and rhythmical, as if dancing a half-walking, half-running gait with dignity to hoe his field.

I am not suggesting that I saw with their eyes or felt exactly what they felt, but their world touched me (and my world touched them). I felt it. It was the feeling of it all. That is how I came to see flesh and blood on the bones of Malinowski's skeleton (1922). All of this was important, not so much because I began to make sense of it by analyzing and ordering it, but because it touched me profoundly—made me feel strong, happy, sad, frustrated, angry, tired, drunk, bored, overwhelmed. All of those things.

UNDERSTANDING "THE OTHER"

In a recent article entitled, "Being Affected by the Other," Gilles Bibeau (1990) suggests two meanings or two directions of the word "affect" which, he says, should be used simultaneously: (1) we must be addressed, moved or touched by "the other"; and (2) this is most validly achieved when we have responsive feelings for, become open to and empathetic with, "the other." Only in this way do we come to recognize that people different from ourselves, including ordinary people, have an experienced and developed knowledge of their own and not merely unsubtantiable "belief" (Good, in press). Only in this way can we come to foster health and healthy activity not only from the "outside in" but from the "inside out."

This two-way procedure is important for most professional practice. From a physician's perspective, the patient and the patient's community are usually, in some degree, "the other." Yet we know that the healing process depends on establishing a therapeutic alliance with the patient and the community (Kleinman et al 1978). Such an alliance cannot be built on assumptions but requires community-specific experience and understanding. In Behrhorst's terms, "health and health concerns must be liberated" within the people themselves.

Behrhorst's appreciation of the "other" extended not only to their diverse beliefs and circumstances but also to their expressed priorities. He loved to repeat the story of how, in a distant village, he failed to introduce treatments he thought were needed until he had listened and responded to the people's own prescriptions for health, which were to keep their chickens alive and plant apple trees. "Start with the people," he would say, "with their pains, their worries and their capacities as key factors in how to improve health. Work within the context of local realities, always!"

In an interdisciplinary setting the physician may seem "the other" to anthropologists and vice versa. Anthropologists take pride in communicating across boundaries, but we must question whether we have established a sufficient alliance with medical practitioners to regularly engage in fruitful dialogue and practice "the art of the possible." Anthropologists blame physicians when we are called in at the last moment. We walk in, puff on our pipe, say "wrong!" and walk out. To work together, anthropologists and physicians will have to attend more closely to each other and to the human problems that they both seek to address. The never-to-be-forgotten lesson of Simajuleu and of the Behrhorst program is that when anthropologists and physicians cooperate with the people in an actual community setting, the way to understanding is improved, and results can be both productive and sustainable.

QUESTIONS AS WELL AS ANSWERS

Central to effective international public health is the importance of finding the right questions in any social setting, not merely giving answers to questions we have formulated within our academies or planning offices. Questions are as important as answers. Problem-posing with the people is as important as problem-solving. New questions and problems arise out of the meanings and the circumstances of the people's lives (these are never separate), and help to form their priorities.

The epidemiologist Steven Polgar (1963) claims the practice of international public health suffers from the "fallacy of interchangeable faces." Public health professionals sometimes falsely assume that because something works in one place it is therefore bound to work anyplace else. But different human settings contain different constellations of factors which impinge on the people's health. We may therefore need to ask questions different from those which produced the most relevant answers elsewhere, and to conduct participatory research in the course of cooperative planning and action. Some public health research, at least, must deliberately expect the unexpected and be open to new questions arising in response to revelations received during the process of the study itself.

Not the least question to ask in the course of our research and program formulations is "so what?" In highland Guatemala I was repeatedly asked about the purpose of our research. Why do we do the research we do? How will the data be used? By whom? For whose benefit? In speaking about improving the health of

African-Americans, the health activist Byllye Avery (1992) recently said bluntly: "Let us not research to death what we already know—let us finally agree to look at what really matters and get on with it." But seeing "what really matters" exactly requires us to ask, deliberately and often, the "so what?" question. This question needs asking even when we are trying to consider the larger context, and even when we are treating what seem unexceptionable topics such as poverty or violence.

Is the motive behind our work to strengthen an academic argument or improve our academic status? Is it to alleviate afflictions we see in the people? Or is it to add to their capacity to pose and deal with problems on their own? Do we really give greater voice and capacity to the subjects through our studies and proposals or do we rob them of both (Chambers 1983, Rogers 1979)?

CONCLUSION—THE ECOLOGICAL PERSPECTIVE

In Simajuleu the multifactoral etiology of disease became inescapable. Disease could actually be seen as "dis-ease" within a series of anatomical, physical, economic, social, political and cultural environments. In considering these interrelated contexts of people's lives, different vectors of disease and sources of "insults" come to light. Social exploitation, poverty and lack of land come to be seen as clear and unmistakable causes of ill health. In the film documentary, "Seeds of Health" (1976), Behrhorst bends over a young boy suffering from one of many bouts with an infectious illness and offers an unusual but sound prescription: "If we are going to heal this little fellow, we must help his family get more land."

If social change is required for saving lives and preserving health, it follows that those pursuing health should be prepared for special difficulties and even potential dangers (Heggenhougen 1984, Stark 1985, Werner and Bower 1982). Francisco Curruchiche, the village health promoter with whom I lived in the village of Simajuleu, together with his son Serafino, were among the many who "disappeared" as a consequence of becoming community leaders and attempting to foster social changes for improved health (Heggenhougen 1984, see Zwi and Ugalde 1989).

A consultation with the health promoter at Simajuleu.

What changes should be attempted by the people, the dimensions and strategies of change, must be decided by the people themselves. It is not for outsiders to judge the propriety or adequacy of actions taken by people in their own community and in their own land. It is important to acknowledge, however, that violence comes in many forms. "The equivalent of 20 nuclear bombs explodes every year in the world of underdevelopment without making a sound," says Vincente Navarro (1984). The silence attending this taken-for-granted violence of preventable deaths from hunger, diarrhea and infectious diseases, and the violence of misery resulting from social, national and international inequities, is deafening. Violence is also present when, in the course of "helping" people, their convictions or their objectives are ignored, passed over or destroyed. For on this their common life and common action depend, including their ability to pose and resolve new problems as they arise.

Health clearly entails consideration of social justice and of equity in the sharing of basic resources. This was a theme of the Alma-Ata declaration on primary health care adopted in 1978 by world health leaders, who drew from the Chimaltenango experience. It is acknowledged in reports of the United Nations (Carstairs 1990) which now monitor development on a multi-factored index. Health and healthy development in a society may require reaffirmation of preexisting social values. We are reminded that the average pre-Columbian Mayan ate better and lived longer than their descendents do today (Behar 1974).

The question arises, Do outsiders have any right to interfere? One answer may be found by referring to ample examples of economically driven interference of the most disastrous kind, which often includes cultural interference that can confuse, disrupt and debilitate. But that would be an insufficient and evasive answer to what is really the wrong question. A better question is to ask, as Behrhorst did, *how* outsiders can most appropriately join and support — and perhaps more widely contextualize — a people's struggle to bring about required changes for health.

The Behrhorst answer lay in lending an outsider's special abilities and skills to be guided, reshaped, used and assumed by local communities themselves in addressing their problems. By learning from "the other," he was able to join his Kaqchikel neighbors on their road to health. He became a key ingredient in their achievement of new and lasting improvements for themselves. He laughed and cried with them and dedicated a mature lifetime of dedicated work to their cause, which had become his cause as well. He left not only a world of friends but a legacy of joining community struggles for health.

References

Avery, B.
  1992 Comments following the presentation of "Miss Evers' Boys" (The Tuskegee Project). Harvard Medical School, April 9, 1992.
Behar, M.
  1974 Malnutrition and Infection—A Deadly Combination. World Health Feb.-March:28-33.
Bibeau, G.
  1990 Being Affected by the Other. Culture, Medicine and Psychiatry 14:299-310.
Capra, F.
  1976 The Tao of Physics. New York: Bantam.
  1982 The Turning Point. London: Flamingo.
Carstairs, J.
  1990 UNDP's New Measure of Development Success. Development Journal 2:40-46.
Chambers, R.
  1983 Whose Knowledge? In: Rural Development: Putting the Last First. R. Chambers, ed. London: Longman.
Dunn, F.L. and C.R. Janes
  1986 Introduction: Medical Anthropology and Epidemiology. In: Anthropology and Epidemiology. C. R. Janes et al, eds. Pp. 3-34. Dordrecht: Reidel Publ. Co.
Engel, G.
  1977 The Need for a New Biomedical Model: A Challenge for Biomedicine. Science 196:129-36.
Good, B.
  In press Medicine, Rationality and Experience: An Anthropological Perspective. Cambridge: Cambridge University Press.

Heggenhougen, H.K.
  1984 Will Primary Health Care be allowed to Succeed? Social
        Science and Medicine 19(3):217-24.
  1992 The Inseparability of Reason and Emotion in the
        Anthropological Perspective: Perceptions upon Leaving 'the
        Field'. In: The Naked Anthropologist: Tales from around the
        World. P.R. DeVita, ed. Belmont, Cal.: Wadsworth.
Kaufert, P.A.
  1990 The 'Box-ification' of Culture: The Role of the Social Scientist.
        Sante, Culture, Health 7(2-3):139-48.
Kleinman, A., L. Eisenberg and B. Good
  1978 Culture, Illness and Care: Clinical Lessons from Anthropologic
        and Cross-cultural Research. Annals of Internal Medicine 99:25-
        58.
Malinowski, B.
  1922 Argonauts of the Western Pacific. Prospect Heights, IL:
        Waveland Press. (Reissued 1984.)
Nations, M.
  1986 Epidemiological Research on Infectious Disease: Quantitative
        Rigor or Rigor Mortis? Insights from Ethnomedicine. In:
        Anthropology and Epidemiology. C. Janes et al, eds. Pp. 97-
        123. Dordrecht: Reidel.
Navarro, V.
  1984 A Critique of the Ideological and Political Positions of the Willy
        Brandt Report and the WHO Alma-Ata Declaration. Social
        Science and Medicine 18:467-74.
Paul, B.
  1955 Health, Culture and Community. New York: Russell Sage.
Polgar, S.
  1963 Health Action in Cross-cultural Perspective. In: Handbook of
        Medical Sociology. H. Freeman, S. Levine and L. Reeder eds.
        Englewood Cliffs: Prentice Hall.
Ramalingaswami, V.
  1986 The Art of the Possible. Social Science and Medicine 22:1097-
        103.
Roger, B.
  1978 Research as Imperialism. CERES March/April:28-31.
Stark, R.
  1985 Lay Workers in Primary Health Care: Victims in the Process of
        Social Transformation. Social Science and Medicine 20(3):269-
        75.

Werner, D. and B. Bower
    1982 Introduction. Warning. Why this Book is so Political. In:
          Helping Health Workers Learn. D. Werner and B. Bower eds.
          Pp. 1-12. Palo Alto, Cal.: Hesperian Foundation.
Zwi, A. and A. Ugalde (eds.)
    1989 Political Violence and Health in the Third World. Social Science
          & Medicine 28(7):entire issue.

12

LESSONS FOR A GRADUATE IN A BATTERED RED JEEP

Jonathan C. Horton

We agreed to meet in front of Doña Luisa's restaurant in Antigua at exactly 7:00 the next morning. It was Friday, 3 February 1984, according to the faded entry in my journal. Dr. Carroll Behrhorst was going to give me a ride to Chimaltenango to show me the clinic. Just the week before, I had arrived from Boston. My plan was to stay in Antigua for a few weeks to work at Spanish before starting work. But I was eager to begin seeing patients as soon as possible.

I arrived a few minutes after seven o'clock. The doctor's red jeep was nowhere in sight. I stood at the curb, scanning the dusty cars rolling along the cobblestone street. The minutes ticked by. The morning air felt fresh and delicious. In the shade it was still cool. After a while, I began to wonder whether Doc had forgotten me. I felt unsure what to do next. Suddenly the door to Doña

Luisa's opened and a young girl emerged. She flashed a brief smile and said softly, «*Ya se fue, el doctor*» (the doctor's already gone). Her hand opened with a crumpled note written in an oversized scrawl: "Can't wait—see you there."

That was my first lesson from Doc. His casual friendliness belied the purposefulness of a man with commitments and an urgent agenda. He had come precisely at 7:00 and waited for one minute. When I failed to appear he did not hesitate to proceed alone. I trudged across town and found a seat on a decorated Bluebird bus headed for Chimaltenango. After disembarking I was carried by the crowd to the central square. The clinic was at the corner near a rebuilt colonial cathedral. The red jeep was parked in front.

It was a market day in Chimaltenango and Doc was too busy to talk. Almost a hundred patients were waiting in the courtyard to see him. A Guatemalan physician gave me a tour of the clinic. With my school Spanish, I strained to catch every word. I was introduced to dozens of people and forgot every name. In the last room I met a beautiful young nurse named Lidia Mucia. I made sure to ask her to write her name down on a scrap of paper. That piece of paper is still glued to the page in my journal marked "3 February 1984."

For the next five months I worked side by side with Carroll Behrhorst. The political violence of the preceding years had cut off the stream of medical students from the United States. I was the only other North American at the clinic. Doc was glad to have the help. I was about to receive an education that would profoundly affect the results of my previous schooling. I here recount some of the lessons.

CLINICAL LESSONS

The doctor had a unique bond with the highland Maya of Guatemala. He knew and admired their cultural traditions. He recognized their places of origin with just a glance at the women's clothing and physiognomy. He would flash a warm grin to arriving strangers and make some reference to their town, as if welcoming strangers from a famous city.

I discovered the strength of this culturally informed approach to patients one Saturday morning when Doc's consultation was interrupted by an emergency call from Antigua. He had to leave immediately, despite the fact that more than thirty patients were still waiting to be seen. I felt immensely pleased when he asked me to finish the morning clinic. To my chagrin, the crowd of people melted away as word spread that the doctor had left early. The receptionist, Ofelia, did her best to advertise me as a very experienced doctor and even managed to promote a rumor that I might be related to Doc. Her effort was to no avail. The faith that patients had in Doc was not easily transferred to anyone else.

Doc was the quintessential general practitioner. He could do everything: drain abscesses, suture wounds, pull teeth, deliver babies, set bones and so on. He also knew the tropical diseases that remain unfamiliar to American physicians. He was superb at recognizing clinical signs and arriving quickly at a sure diagnosis. When in doubt, he used empiric treatment. Usually it worked.

He knew the solution to clinical problems I had never encountered before. One morning a mother brought her three-year-old child to the clinic with a report that the youngster had stuffed a kernel of dry corn up his nose. I could see nothing when I looked up the nostril with a speculum. I reassured the mother that nothing was wrong, but a few days later she returned. The child's nose was swollen and draining yellow mucous. I tried to clear the nasal passage by probing blindly with a surgical clamp. I got nowhere. The child screamed and fought and the nose began to bleed. I told the mother to see Dr. Behrhorst. The next day she returned with her child. The boy began to cry as soon as he saw me. Doc grabbed the child and waited to time his move. As the child began to wail, Doc pinched closed the patent nostril, placed his mouth over the child's mouth, and exhaled a great breath. The kernel of corn wrapped in a wad of mucous came flying out of the nose.

Doc mobilized patients in their own behalf. While seeing a patient he would carefully explain the diagnosis, the rationale behind his prescribed treatment and the healing roles to be

Available tool.

assumed by both patients and their families. Usually a short lecture was offered in front of the family and any other listeners sitting in the waiting room. If the patient had to be admitted to the hospital, family members were encouraged to remain for care and support. Cooking and laundry facilities were available in the yard. At night family members slept on mats on the floor, clustered around the patient's cot. When the mountain air was cold, the doors and windows were tightly shuttered so the wards remained warm with the heat generated by all the people packed inside.

BROADER APPLICATIONS

The Mayan peoples have never enjoyed ready access to professional health care in Guatemala. Most of the health care resources are concentrated in Guatemala City, where hospitals are quite modern, including units that offer open-heart surgery, renal dialysis, neonatal intensive care and other tertiary services. The nation has invested little sustained effort and few dependable resources to making health care available in rural areas. In the 1970s the Ministry of Health constructed an ambitious system of 600 health posts. These buildings, neatly whitewashed and emblazoned with the letters *Puesto de Salud*, can still be spotted while passing through villages in the countryside, but they are now mostly empty and closed. Civil strife and economic crises have caused the government to cut health expenditures by 60 percent during the past decade. Most of these posts are now abandoned; the remainder are open for only a few hours a day.

In larger towns, where private doctors and hospitals are available, few of the people can afford them. Children die because families cannot scrape together the funds to get through the door. To save money families often shop for their own remedies at local pharmacies, where the pharmacist may offer a few words of free advice. It is worth adding that in Guatemala pharmaceuticals are a good business. Medicines sell at the same prices as in the United States or at slightly higher prices. Roosevelt Avenue, the main artery leading into Guatemala City, is lined with modern, nicely landscaped corporate headquarters representing all the major drug manufacturers in the world.

Doc knew that his patients wished to be self-sufficient, even though they were poor, and knew that self-sufficiency is a mark of health. His goal at the clinic was to keep things as simple as possible. He listened to the people, learned about their life and figured out how best to assist them. To arrive at a diagnosis he relied almost entirely on a careful history and physical examination. He did not believe in ordering unnecessary laboratory tests. By design he limited laboratory services to a minimum: blood count, urine and stool analysis, tests for acid-fast bacteria, Gram's staining and malaria smears.

He asked critical questions about some medical technologies. While I was at the clinic, Doc was offered a Coulter counter by a sympathetic American hospital administrator. He refused the gift, though he knew that a Coulter counter was a thousand times faster than a lab technician with a hemocytometer. He saw the more sophisticated instrument as a trap. It would consume expensive reagents, require regular servicing and simply encourage the ordering of more blood tests by the hospital staff. On one occasion we unpacked together a shipment of medical supplies from the United States. It contained endotracheal tubes, central venous lines, disposable needles and syringes, and similar paraphernalia. As we broke into each box Doc's expression grew more quizzical. It was obvious that he would have preferred antibiotics, bandages and thermometers.

Doc judged that more lives could be saved and more health fostered by making cheap, basic care available to everyone. He viewed this as preferable to providing more expensive, advanced care to only a few who could pay the price. In the vocabulary of contemporary experts in medical economics, he tried to provide "cost effective" procedures. The most common diseases were dehydration, diarrhea, respiratory infection, parasites and malnutrition, for which effective, low-cost treatment is available. To extract maximum benefit from limited resources, Doc emphasized the efficient use of vaccines, antibiotics, anthelmintics and rehydration solutions.

Lidia Mucia with patients at the Chimaltenango clinic.

From the perspective of the Mayan patient, doctors seem deprecating and impatient. Many such patients speak little Spanish and feel intimidated trying to explain themselves. To them, hospitals are not only expensive but unfriendly places. Doc was aware that all these factors combined to create barriers.

The belief is widely held that the "developing" world lacks an adequate supply of doctors, but Doc viewed physicians as an expensive solution to many health problems. He recognized that doctors, equipped with their elaborate diagnostic procedures and medical therapies, have not been able to improve the availability of medical care to the world's poor. Increasingly, Doc came to believe that it was not feasible to solve the health problems of Guatemala by using physicians as primary health care providers.

To solve these problems, he recruited promising workers from local communities and trained them himself, in some instances providing scholarships for them to attend nursing school. In this way he built a dedicated staff of competent Kaqchikel nurses. Some worked with him for more than twenty years. Occasionally a nurse married an American medical student and left the clinic to move to the United States. Over the years in Chimaltenango this cost the clinic six nurses. Doc viewed this staff attrition with good humor—perhaps because he had done the very same thing in marrying his beloved wife, Alicia.

Doc found that he could run the hospital efficiently by sharing responsibility with the nursing staff. They often made important decisions in the management of care for individual patients, and they directed special programs in nutrition, family planning, sanitation and tuberculosis control. Ironically, as he came to this understanding, hundreds of new patients were drawn to the outpatient clinic. This, of course, turned him more intentionally toward work in the villages.

RELAXED BEHIND THE WHEEL

Doc loved to drive and talk. During my stay in Guatemala, we made weekly visits to towns where he had established agricultural or water projects or satellite assessment clinics. Doc would relax and become loquacious behind the wheel. After 25 years he knew a lot about Guatemala. He could tell you that the ceiba tree, the national tree of Guatemala, is actually larger than the California redwood if measured in terms of foliage surface area rather than height. He knew the trading patterns and goods produced by every town. He was always waving to people along the route, as if he were acquainted with half the roadside population of Guatemala.

At times our conversation moved to heavy subjects. From 1978 to 1983, when political violence had fallen like a plague on Chimaltenango, killings in the countryside became a daily event and many people that Doc had trained became targets. He felt anguish at all the deaths, but he felt a personal measure of responsibility for the deaths of health workers associated with the clinic. He pondered decisions the foundation had made and turned them over and over in his mind. But he never felt the clinic should close its doors. Those conversations will always echo in my mind.

I returned to the United States just a few days before graduation from medical school in June, 1984. I attended the ceremony but felt dispirited and lost amid all the pomp and self-congratulation. After five months in Guatemala one's perspective is changed. In December, 1984, Lidia Mucia and I were married in Patzún, Guatemala. We stayed in touch with Doc but he was a terrible correspondent. At the bottom of his stationery stood a quotation from Mark Twain: "I put off answering letters for at least six months—by that time you'd be surprised how many don't need answering."

I saw him for the last time in November, 1989, while attending a medical meeting in New Orleans. He seemed restless before dinner and suggested that we drive over to Tulane to pick up some papers. As we drove downtown we began to talk just as we did on our drives through the Guatemalan countryside. When we got to the office Doc couldn't find the papers he was looking for.

It didn't seem to matter much. We had enjoyed a good talk together.

Five years before, we had driven together on the South Coast of Guatemala to visit a finca in Chicacao where he had established a health program. We became so engrossed in conversation that Doc drove past the road leading to the farm. We drove another 20 miles to the outskirts of Mazatenango before he realized his mistake and turned around. In our home Lidia and I have a wall map of Guatemala on which I have marked in black ink all the roads I have traveled in that country. The map looks like a giant spider web, with Antigua and Chimaltenango at the center. Along Route CA-2 on the south coast is drawn a small spur, 20 miles long, which simply comes to a stop. So has the life of Doc, which followed many spurs in the course of educating us all for revisions of medicine and medical education which must now take place in many more places. When I look at the map, I smile and remember that day with Doc at the wheel driving and talking while I was learning in his battered red jeep.

13

COMBATING MEASLES IN THE HIGHLANDS

Nigel Paneth

I still have the *cuaderno para copias*, the little notebook with the colorful Mayan blouse design on the front cover and arithmetic tables on the back, purchased twenty years ago in San Martín Jilotepeque. On these pages were entered the details of our plan to immunize 5,000 children between the ages of one and six against measles in the highland villages surrounding San Martín.

In the manner of people who had never undertaken such an enterprise before, we scrupulously listed our resources: 171 glass syringes and eight of plastic; 145 reusable needles sorted by size; bandages, alcohol, cotton, vaccination cards, tweezers, ice, stationery and authorization forms. Several hundred vials of Schwartz-type attenuated measles vaccine had been donated by a Louisiana parish to the government of Guatemala, which in turn had handed it over to the government's twelve highland rural clinics. With only modest guidance from the health authorities, each clinic was left to its own devices in organizing a local vaccination campaign.

Band for a feast day or for an immunization.

The clinics were at that time staffed by a few poorly paid nurses and a rotation of usually reluctant medical students from the capital, and constituted virtually the entire government investment in rural health. At our clinic in San Martín just three medicines were in good supply: iron, isoniazid and an anti-helminth — thousands of pills stored in huge glass jars. In the back of the room was a large cardboard box with drug-company samples from which a ten-day course of antibiotic could be strung together if one was not overscrupulous about sticking with one type of medicine.

Our human resources were also listed in the notebook: Enrique and Jorge — two Guatemalan medical students performing their one-month required rural service; Alicia, Dorotea, Huberta — nurses in the San Martín clinic; María Teresa — our nutritionist from Costa Rica, inventor of numerous INCAPARINA recipes;[1] Eliodoro, Felix, Faustino, and Timoteo — who were Behrhorst clinic health promoters. A note says that Rogelio Bunch will lend us a car for three days, another that we can count on catechists for publicity. I was a medical student from the United States doing a two-month elective in tropical medicine with INCAP, assigned to work in San Martín.

We began our vaccination campaign with an *acta de inauguración*, a kickoff celebration held, the notebook informs me, at nine o'clock in the morning, Tuesday, February 22, 1972, in San Martín's main square. It begins with a parade of school children, is followed by speeches from medical student Enrique, then the mayor, the priest, Behrhorst *promotor* Felix Balán, representatives of the voluntary organizations *Acción Conjunta* and *Vecinos Mundiales*, and the local heads of education and of public health. It ends with a *vacunación symbólica* or first performance. (The notes say to get a band, flowers, students, five tables, 15 chairs and a microphone.) A large crowd was attracted to the sunny plaza that morning and waited patiently for the speeches to end, at which point we began our vaccinations right there on the square and did not move from it for three more days.

---

[1] A high-protein food supplement developed by INCAP (the Central American Institute of Nutrition in Guatemala City) for improving nutritional status, especially in pregnant and lactating women and in children.

The highlands were then experiencing a rare interlude of peace. A nine o'clock curfew had recently been lifted in the villages. I was told by a United States medical student who had recently been to the highlands that, during his two-month elective, three Mayan men had been shot dead in Chimaltenango for the crime of being too intoxicated to know what time it was. At the time of our visit soldiers stood guard with automatic weapons at every building and bank — a sign of forces yet to be unleashed.

The time of our visit, too, was a brief moment of amicable relations among the several groups involved in highland health. Although my affiliation was with INCAP and with a government-sponsored clinic, no medical student, nurse or doctor who found themselves in the highlands could be kept very long from the *hospitalito* in Chimaltenango. There was too much to learn from Carroll Behrhorst, who found a use for each and every one of us. One day, as I was just passing through, he grabbed my arm and said: "Ever sewn up an artery? Come over here." We all learned quickly the basic Behrhorst themes for health care among the Kaqchikel — the deep respect for the Mayan way of life, the desperate need for land reform, the central role of the indigenous promoters. We also saw how modest resources could be translated into effective medical care.

On another visit to Chimaltenango I was recruited to provide a highland tour for a distinguished visitor from New York. Never-mind that I myself had lately arrived in the highlands. The long drive in Doc's jeep, including the usual visit to Chichicastenango, allowed us to reflect on Berhrhorstian precepts. Thus, when the word came that a measles vaccination campaign was in the offing in San Martín, we knew that we would be working cooperatively and that we would be looking to Doc as a model to follow.

We were, I think, the only highland clinic in that campaign to take our vaccination show on the road. We covered sixteen main villages. We set up a total of 52 vaccination stations on fincas, in hamlets or at road junctions. The sounds of the place names will resonate with all who have spent time in the Central American highland — Choabajito, Pacoj, Xesuj, Semetabaj, Quimal, Pachaj. We broke up into groups of two or three and moved from one place to another, vaccinating for as long as parents brought their children, which was often late into the night. When villages could not be reached by car, we employed mules and donkeys to get to our destinations.

The enthusiastic response of the Kaqchikel people to our efforts continues to astonish me even now. In it was reflected the dread fear of *sarampión* (measles), which brings death to malnourished children. Mortality statistics testified to the lethality of this disease, so rarely fatal in industrialized societies. But also reflected in the response was the gentle love and concern of Kaqchikel parents for their children, which made for a surprising acceptance of at least some aspects of Western medicine.

TWO FACES OF MEDICINE

Clearly, medicine as practiced in Chimaltenango and San Martín was not exactly what I had learned in Boston. Harvard left so much out! I realized from my highland experience how narrow a definition of medicine I had been given. I had suspected this before, but the experience of those two months gave substance to my suspicion that medicine needed a broader perspective, one that took account of the context — socioeconomic and environmental — in which illness arose.

Much was to be learned about the Mayan people from the way in which they dealt with the crises that disease brought. On my first day in San Martín, a memorable Monday, a middle-aged woman was brought in by her husband. Because she could not walk, he had strapped her to a chair and tied the chair to his back. He was no bigger than she and he had carried her this way for three hours, much of his walk uphill. She had a rare condition in the highlands — hypertension.

Later that same day, a feverish and convulsive child of five was brought in by his father. I was alone (it was still Monday and Guatemala City medical students stretched out their weekend as long as they could) but I quelled my rising panic sufficiently to ask for an anticonvulsant. Some shuffling in the back and a two milliliter vial of phenobarbital was produced. Somehow I found a vein and gave a hefty amount (I was too nervous to carefully calculate

A health promoter teaches his children the proper use of syringes.

the dose), eventually controlling the seizure but also putting the child into a deep sleep. As I paced around the clinic wondering whether I had done the child irreparable harm, his father placed his hand on my shoulder and whispered «*cálmate*» (relax).

Enrique and Jorge then arrived and showed me how to use the two-way radio to arrange transportation for the child to the hospital in Antigua. I was still genuinely worried that the child might be so stuporous that he would stop breathing on the way. "Not with roads like these," said the knowledgeable Enrique. A few days later, dad and son paid us a visit and thanked me for my efforts. This was one of many instances when I thought it was I who should do the thanking.

The clinic was busy with patients and my responses alternated between frustration and exhilaration. For the teenager whose eyes were beginning to weaken from onchocerciasis, commonly called river blindness, all I could do was remove the larger cysts, knowing that it would do little good. Only a broader environmental approach could conquer this disease; and even that would help only the next generation. On one occasion a woman was carried down the mountainside who had just breathed her last after hemorrhaging from delivery. The motherless baby's fate was at best a question mark. Only a system providing skilled assistance close to the places of delivery could avert such tragic outcomes.

Yet most patients in the clinic were testimony to the good that can be accomplished through a very modest sharing of basic technology and resources. Young adults with serious abscesses managed effectively with application of a clean scalpel and a few days of antibiotics. Dehydrated infants too weak to suckle were saved by nasogastric tube feedings. Intestinal parasites were held at bay, at least temporarily, by medication. Machete injuries found treatment which, left untreated, could have led to death through blood loss.

I saw Doc the day before I was to leave Guatemala. He looked at me bemusedly as if to say, why would anyone want to leave this paradise? One striking aspect of Doc's commitment to the highlands was his genuine enjoyment of what he was doing and of being where he was. He never seemed to be fulfilling an obligation or even a mission. He carried none of the severity and seriousness one sees in photographs of Albert Schweitzer. Usually he just seemed to be having the time of his life, as if no other work could ever be so much fun or so fulfilling. This too was a Carroll Behrhorst lesson. Enjoy what you do and you will do it well.

He told me then that I would be back. I haven't yet returned to the highlands; but Doc was right in that my mind is often there. In 1976, as a pediatric resident at Jacobi Hospital in the Bronx, I was shocked by the news of the devastation caused by the earthquake. I learned from the foundation newsletter that San Martín had been at the epicenter of the quake, that more than a thousand of its ten thousand residents were dead, that hardly a building was left standing. I wondered over and over how many members of our vaccination team had been hurt or killed. In searching for ways to help, my instinct was to trust Carroll Behrhorst, secure in the knowledge that funds contributed to the clinic would be well spent.

For medical students interested in public health but not wanting to disentangle themselves completely from curative medicine there have been few models. These two faces of medicine—Hygeia and Aesculapius—have rarely coexisted easily, especially not in the same person or program. What I found in the Guatemalan highlands was not a classical public health program, nor was it conventional medicine. It took the best of two different worlds and blended them to synthesize something better than either. In this it has afforded a model for many, including myself.

After pediatric training I studied epidemiology at Columbia, and since then my academic appointments have straddled the two disciplines. Most of my work has been devoted to the application of epidemiologic concepts to pediatric problems, particularly infant mortality and childhood neurologic handicap. It was in Guatemala that I decided to become a pediatrician, and that is where I also saw the power, both actual and potential, of public health initiatives. Looking back, I often wonder whether, in the course of my pediatric practice through the years, so much benefit has accrued to so many children as occurred during those few days of combating measles in the highlands.

14

GAINS IN CHILD SURVIVAL
THROUGH SOCIAL MOBILIZATION

William H. Foege

The last 30 years of Carroll Behrhorst's life were productive years, dedicated to the health of people for whom rapid scientific and medical developments are not the norm and are often out of reach. A half-century ago when he received his schooling and training, it was uncommon to find mentors who believed significant changes were possible in the less "developed" areas of the world. Yet Behrhorst went forth to learn what could and should be done.

Here we wish to ask: What has been the collective impact on the health of children by those who have responded to a similar call? Behrhorst might be surprised, but he would also be pleased to note some of the results.

Recess at Xajaxac, Sololá, Guatemala: Child survival is for life.

THIRTY YEARS OF PROGRESS

Infant Mortality

The collective infant mortality for the globe was 127 deaths for every 1,000 live births in 1960. That figure covered vast inequities at the time, as does the average figure today. Nonetheless, the global figure in 1990 was less than 70, and the number of countries with an infant mortality rate over 150 dropped from 48 countries in 1960 to less than five in 1990.

Life Expectancy

In 1960, 24 countries had a life expectancy at birth that was below 40 years. Not a single country was still in that category in 1990. In 1960 there were 60 countries with a life expectancy at birth of less than 50 years. In 1990 less than 20 countries still had such discouraging figures. The global life expectancy has now increased to about 60 years at birth and will approach 65 by the end of the century.

Birth Rates

The world still needs to face up to the catastrophic problems resulting from the exploding world population, the overconsumption of resources per person and the resulting degradation of the environment. If there is any good news in this fateful scenario, it is that birth rates are beginning to decline in many places around the world. A surprising reduction in birth rates has been recorded in China and in other Asian countries. Less spectacular reductions are taking place in Latin America and even Africa is beginning to see the first signs of change.

In recent years, moreover, evidence has accumulated to show that improvements in infant and child survival are actually associated with a decline in birthrates rather than with a simple increase in population, as many had feared. It is now possible to envision and devote energies to a dual reduction of both birthrates and childhood diseases.

Specific Diseases

In addition to this overall improvement in the health picture, the past 30 years have witnessed some spectacular changes in the incidence of particular diseases.

Smallpox. — In response to a program launched in 1966 by the World Health Organization, the countries of the world were able to organize themselves effectively for the first time to achieve a global objective. A total of forty-three countries reported smallpox in 1966, but through collective action and a sharing of resources the final natural case of smallpox was recorded in Somalia in October 1977. The world now celebrates fifteen years of freedom from the first disease ever eliminated by the cooperative planning and action of people.

Measles. — By 1990 the global immunization program, which built on the successes of smallpox eradication, had penetrated all countries of the world and most villages and hamlets of those countries. Between 1984 and 1990 the immunization coverage of children in developing countries increased from less than 20 percent to 80 percent. This reduced the incidence of the target diseases. In 1990, two million children did *not* die of measles who would have done so on previous trends — a remarkable change in the course of a disease that has historically robbed young families of their hopes and futures.

Diarrhea. — So ubiquitous that it is seen by many as an expected part of growing up, diarrhea drains the life from five million children a year. Now a change is in the offing. With the discovery and demonstration that oral rehydration can maintain the life of most children and adults during times of diarrhea, the primary challenge has become one of finding ways to get this simple technology to every village in such a way that it will actually be used. In 1990, if we compare numbers with earlier years, one million children were spared a diarrhea death. The way has been paved to increase that figure to two and one-half million children saved per year by the end of the century.

TRENDS

During the past 125 years private groups, especially church-related groups, have provided a foundation for international health efforts. An early child survival initiative was conceived and launched by a national agency, the U.S. Agency for International Development. Increasingly, however, agencies of the United Nations Organization, especially the World Health Organization and the United Nations Children's Fund, are providing the global objectives, vision and umbrella for international health efforts. Bilateral agencies continue to contribute large amounts of financial assistance but usually in conformity with plans developed by the UN agencies. A healthy collaboration has developed, beginning with immunizations, which is improving the effectiveness of international health activities.

This improvement in international collaboration has been matched by cooperation at national and local levels. Social mobilization, as it is now often called, engages entire communities and all their organizations in improving health possibilities for their children. Local churches, police, radio stations, parents groups and commercial establishments all contribute resources for immunization days and for ongoing health programs.

A very encouraging sign is the broad political interest that has developed for child survival programs. Many examples are available of national leaders who advertise immunization and other child survival programs, and who even take an active part in immunizing children themselves. A high point was reached on September 30, 1990, when 71 heads of state convened at the UN building in New York to set objectives for child survival and child health to be reached by the year 2000. There has never been a more important year for the survival of children worldwide than 1990.

FUTURE CHALLENGES

Behrhorst would be pleased by the recounting of these improvements but he would also be conscious of how much is left to be done. Better ways must be found both of preserving local communities and of producing global citizens — people who ask concerning proposed innovations, What would be the impact on communities everywhere? If it is good for the world, it is likely ultimately to be good for the nation and for our own community. Healthy children are good for the world as a whole — and worldwide child health is also good for each community.

The next years should see a strengthening of world organizations. This is not only a way of making certain that global concerns are present in our thinking but also a way of posing global objectives that might otherwise never be attempted or reached. It is clear that smallpox eradication would not simply have happened over time. It had to be focused as a global objective and the world had to be mobilized in new ways to make that objective achievable.

Finally, there is a challenge to exploit scientific efforts for the improvement of health rather than for mass destruction. Perhaps health concerns will never compete successfully with military concerns, but the effort must be made to use our science, our talents and our resources for preserving life and enhancing its quality.

15

PARTICIPATORY HEALTH FOR REFUGEES
"Start with What They Know"

Patricia O'Connor and Brian Leo Treacy

Displacement across political borders is taking place on a large scale in many places around the world. Many of those displaced are from the world's poorest communities. The United Nations High Commissioner for Refugees (UNHCR) estimates that there are more than 100,000 refugees in Latin America (not including those, mostly from Central America, who fled their countries for the United States by the thousands during the 1980s), that more than half a million refugees are scattered across Asia, and that five to six million people in Africa have fled hunger or violence in their homelands.

We have worked with groups of refugees in the United States, Central America and East Africa, where our responsibilities have been in the areas of public health and legal protection. Much of the impulse and vision that we bring to our work was gained

Guatemalan families plan for nutrition and child care with a nurse of the clinic in Chimaltenango.

during a decade of association with Carroll Behrhorst, whom we met in 1980 and 1982, respectively. Those were difficult years for the foundation and for the doctor personally. Death and destruction ripped through the highlands, leaving families and communities devastated. Tens of thousands of Guatemalans, mostly Maya, fled to Mexico, and as many as 200,000 more were internally displaced and went into hiding in other areas of Guatemala. Untold thousands were killed or disappeared. Massacres of adult males sometimes left entire communities of widows and children.

For a time, much of the foundation's work in rural communities virtually ceased. When the work revived, Doc provided leadership to make sure that it proceeded according to the basic principles of community development that had been established earlier. To us, two gringos from Louisiana, the rural situation seemed desperate —woeful shortages of food, clothing, housing, agricultural tools and seeds. Though we knew the best approach with displaced people was to balance short-term survival with longer-term processes of community preservation and development, we did not know how to proceed.

Doc viewed recovery from the violence in Guatemala much as he viewed recovery from the earthquake. Working with him and others, we came to understand that communities living in the wake of profound disruption are highly vulnerable not only to trauma and disease but also to the formation of new dependencies. It would have been comparatively easy for us to design programs of immediate response with the single goal of distributing food, clothing and medicines to the refugees. But rather than turn troubled, vulnerable people into recipients of programs that simply dump relief supplies and walk away, we tried to work from a broader concept. Survivors of violence would be encouraged to define their own problems and to activate their own strategies for physical, emotional, social and economic recovery —a more complicated and longer-term process.

As we moved from Guatemala to other refugee-producing situations, we encountered again and again the difficulties that lie in the way of putting this idea into practice. The helping agencies —the donors and the organizations that deliver services (food, medical assistance, housing and school materials)—typically also deliver an externally derived view of health problems and their solution. In the best case, a few refugee volunteers are recruited as laborers to construct latrines or prepare and serve food. But refugees ordinarily have little role in defining their own needs or in setting up the programs that are to meet them.

This state of affairs is detrimental because, in the short term, it misses an opportunity to make difficult circumstances more tolerable for refugees by making use of their ideas on how best to cope with health problems in a new environment. Over the long term, attempts to impose a health care system that ignores the shared beliefs of refugees about health and sickness will also threaten their cultural survival. Already rendered vulnerable by their uprootedness, refugee groups would appear to deserve special efforts to create a participatory framework.

A combination of elements in refugee settings renders such community participation particularly elusive. Special difficulties are traceable to the unique nature of refugee populations, to a dependence of the assistance agencies on government donations and to donor interest in visible short term impact. These considerations merit inspection along the way to asking whether and how a major deficit in addressing refugee health problems can be corrected.

THE UNIQUE NATURE OF REFUGEE POPULATIONS

The high morbidity and mortality that are common in refugee enclosures arise from four fundamental changes in the epidemiological base: (1) the loss or breakdown of a previous health infrastructure, (2) the movement of populations into new ecological zones where there are new disease risks, (3) the crowded living conditions leading to higher disease transmission rates, and (4) the high incidence of malnutrition causing increased susceptibility to disease (Shears and Lusty 1988). All these factors require immediate consideration and response.

To be effective, this response should be grounded in the refugee community's own belief system, including its ideas about how to stay healthy, why people become ill and what should be done when illness occurs. But refugees are cut off from their places of origin, including the understandings and practices of health that obtain there, and can no longer rely on their customary strategies. They are separated from like-minded support groups such as relatives and friends on whom they formerly relied. Home remedies, traditional healers, pharmacies, community health workers and other familiar options are generally unavailable to them. Instead, they often find themselves housed in camps without any option to leave when sick and with little or no contact with their places of origin.

Many components of a culture, including health beliefs, combine to form an inherently dynamic, supportive and healing system. But the refugee context is by its very nature an environment of stress, which becomes intensified through the imposition of unfamiliar terms and practices.

UNHCR DEPENDENCE UPON DONOR LARGESSE

The UNHCR was created in 1951 by the United Nations General Assembly in response to an anticipated temporary need to assist refugees fleeing Eastern Europe in the aftermath of World War II. The agency was accorded a three-year life span, which has been extended and re-extended so that the UNHCR exists today by virtue of a series of now routine three-year mandates. This agency has never received financial support from the General Assembly, but has conducted its own fund-raising efforts with donor governments. Now, forty years later, the UNHCR has grown in scope to bear primary responsibility for the protection of refugees worldwide and for coordinating international assistance. However, given its temporary charter and its total reliance on donor governments for funding, the UNHCR is predictably compelled to register the kind of rapid results that speak to donors.

In addressing a refugee crisis, the UNHCR's usual procedure is to act quickly, perform centralized planning, maintain high-coverage statistics through large-scale service delivery structures, and utilize its own trained and experienced staff or consultants. The pressure to mount a quick, high-impact relief operation understandably conflicts with the long-term interests of the refugees to share in planning and managing a program suited to their own health priorities. Thus, refugees exercise little influence on health services that are established solely to address their health problems.

DONOR GOVERNMENT INTEREST IN
HIGH-VISIBILITY RESULTS

The first reaction to a movement of refugees is a UNHCR special appeal for emergency funds to address immediate needs in what is frequently described as a life or death situation. This appeal is issued, as a matter of course, to Western donor countries since they are most able to respond with necessary contributions. Hoping to keep the pipeline open, the UNHCR and its implementing partners are no less conscious of the donors' interests than they are of those of the refugees. Hence, a quick-impact program is envisioned. The most secure course seems one which draws upon donor models of health care with which donor-funded service providers are most familiar.

In most instances this implies a tendency to establish a hierarchical model of Western-trained provider and unknowing recipient. The objective is to "deliver" Western medical supplies and services such as food, immunizations and trained medical personnel. The only action required on the part of the refugees themselves is a passive acceptance of the services offered. In participatory health programs, on the other hand, refugees would themselves supply input at every stage of the program — from identifying their problems to devising and administering the strategies that are to address them.

REFUGEE PARTICIPATION IN HEALTH PROGRAMS

An example drawn from the Mosquitia region in Honduras may help illustrate how important refugee participation can be. In 1988, when large numbers of Miskitos from Nicaragua sought refuge in Honduras, twelve young women in one settlement exhibited a series of symptoms which Western-trained physicians were unable to diagnose. The girls displayed cycles of relative calm followed by hyperactivity including shouting, crying and attempts to throw themselves out of windows or into a river. The physicians recognized their inability to treat the women, and did little more than prescribe symptomatic relief through sedatives. Family members and other camp residents knew that the girls could be treated by a traditional healer, but there was none resident in the settlement.

After several such episodes, the community requested and received permission to dispatch a commission of refugees outside the settlement to identify a traditional healer. The commission located a healer, also a Miskito from Nicaragua, who resided near the Nicaragua-Honduras border. The healer's treatment succeeded where the Western medical experts had failed. Because of this success he was persuaded to remain in the camp and continue offering a viable alternative to Western care, one appropriate to problems as identified by the refugees themselves.

Throughout most of the world a medical pluralism is now practiced in which Western and traditional approaches are applied simultaneously, sequentially, or intermittentently (Heggenhougen and Shore 1986; Heggenhougen 1980; Leslie 1977). It would seem that refugee settlements above all should have access to such knowing and flexible care. Despite good intentions, however, the reality remains otherwise. This would require, as our examplefrom the Mosquitia demonstrates, recognizing the merits of traditional approaches to health and then moving collaboratively to build programs around established beliefs and practices. In the end, the only way to achieve participation is to recognize the authority of people to make decisions about their own health and to communicate information that makes informed choices possible.

WHAT TO DO?

What would Behrhorst have seen as an appropriate course of action in these complex situations? Over his desk in the office we

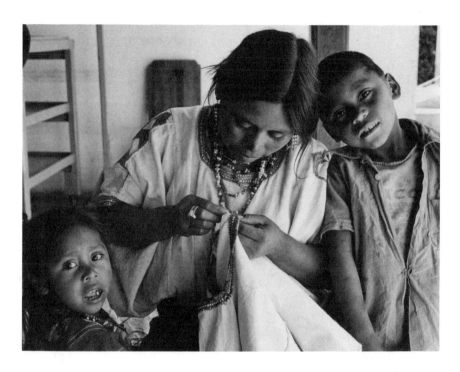

The patient as agent: A mother cares for her children in the hospital at Chimaltenango, Guatemala.

shared at Tulane University hung some lines from the *Tao Te Ching* (perhaps sixth century BCE). They were handwritten by Doc, who often commented that they "said it all." They suggest that a new commitment and a new mode of learning are keys to the answer.

> Go to the people.
> Live with the people.
> Learn from them.
> Love them.

Refugee perceptions and expressions afford useful information and provide a basis for planning appropriate health programs with them.   Resulting activities will incorporate elements of both traditional and Western systems. Individual programs will vary since their content will depend on specific cultural information—special knowledge, attitudes, beliefs and practices.

> Start with what they know.
> Build on what they have.

Participation by refugees means much more than supplying volunteers to fill bottom rungs on a service provision ladder (Welsh 1988). It requires their collaboration in defining problems and achieving solutions at all levels. It requires leaving models behind in which Western-trained personnel behave as though they have more privileged health knowledge and skills than refugee leaders or traditional healers and as though decisions flow from sophisticated providers to unknowledgeable recipients.

It is from this model of decision making that the image emerges of resistant, uncooperative patients. That image is empirically inaccurate. Refugees, like other poor communities around the world, are quick to evaluate the advantages and disadvantages of Western health services—but on their own terms. When they adopt a new procedure or technique they do not necessarily adopt biomedical theories of disease; rather, they interpret these interventions in terms of their customary understandings about health and disease.

When the task is finished
the people will say,
"We did it ourselves."

They must so say, if the end is to be a healthy one. The rapid and at times unpredictable adaptive strategies of refugees necessitated by mass migration are beyond our control. Yet our actions clearly affect the likelihood of their physical and cultural survival. It becomes an ethical responsibility to understand the full consequences of our actions, rather than bow to pressures for quick results by imposing a health delivery system that fosters dependency and displaces competency in people we thought to serve. To disregard the unique ideas and capacities brought along by refugees themselves is to disregard their very health and to impoverish us all.

References

Heggenhougen, H. Kris
    1980   Bomohs, Doctors, and Sinsehs: Medical Pluralism in Malaysia. Social Science and Medicine 14B:235-244.
Heggenhougen, H. Kris and L. Shore
    1986   Cultural Components of Behavioral Epidemiology: Implications for Primary Health Care. Social Science and Medicine 22(11):1-235-1245.
Leslie, Charles M.
    1977   Pluralism and Integration in the Indian and Chinese Medical Systems. In: Culture, Disease and Healing. David Landy (ed.). Pp. 511-517. New York: Macmillan.
Shears, P. and T. Lusty
    1988   Communicable Disease Epidemiology Following Migration: Studies From the African Famine. International Migration Review 11(3):783-795.
Welsh, Robert L.
    1988   Primary Health Care: A Papua New Guinea Example. Cultural Survival Quarterly 12(1):1-4.

16

THE LOCAL COMMUNITY HEALTH BOARD IN FATICK, SENEGAL

Issakha Diallo
Christopher Murrill

Located in the westernmost part of sub-Saharan Africa, Senegal currently has a population of about seven million people, one-fifth of whom live in the capital city region of Dakar. Its economy consists primarily of agriculture, especially peanut production. Since gaining its independence in 1960, Senegal has maintained a politically stable democratic government and continues to have strong ties with France. The official language is French and the organization of the government closely follows that of France.

Like many other African countries, Senegal suffers from a low gross national product ($630 per capita), a low literacy rate (37 percent among men, 19 percent among women), a relatively high population growth rate (2.8 percent) and poor food production caused in part by inadequate soil conditions and limited rainfall.

Fatick is one of ten regions in Senegal and is about the size of the state of Rhode Island, having a surface area of 3,068 square miles consisting primarily of flat terrain. The soil is sandy in the central and northeastern sections and there is swampland in the western section. This region has a population at present of approximately 550,000 persons, including five different ethnic groups. Eighty percent of the population is Muslim and the rest of the people are Roman Catholic or animist. There are mixtures of animism with Muslim and Roman Catholic practices.

Health problems in the region are dominated by a severe infant mortality rate of 112 per 1,000 live births, a preadolescent death rate of 220 per 100,000 and a maternal mortality rate estimated at 850 per 100,000. The average life expectancy in Fatick is 48 years. Infectious, parasitic and nutritional diseases are prevalent, of which cholera and malaria are the most extreme (Ministère de la Santé Publique 1986-1990).

The national government is responsible for public health provisions in Senegal but, as the numbers indicate, it has not been able by itself to improve the poor state of health. On the local level, medical resources (both professionals and trained lay workers) are lacking. Until recently, moreover, there has been little expression, decision making or participation on the part of local communities themselves regarding provisions for health.

ORGANIZING FOR CITIZEN HEALTH ACTIVITY

In the face of these inadequacies and lack of effective governmental programs, the people of Fatick have undertaken initiatives that accord with the principles expounded and practiced in villages of Chimaltenango. The citizens of Fatick have now formed their own board of health consisting of local community members. This board has assumed responsibility for planning and implementing preventive health programs.

In this case the Behrhorst influence extends both from his work in Guatemala and from his teaching of international students in the School of Public Health and Tropical Medicine at Tulane University in New Orleans, where we were grateful learners. His insistence that citizens have a right and responsibility to take charge of their own health spurred the development of the Fatick board of health. His guidelines for public health initiatives among the rural poor helped to shape some of their programs.

Several previous changes in the organization of the Senegalese government facilitated this move. In 1972 local branches of government, composed of ordinary citizens, were formed in the nation's regions. In 1978 the government also adopted a legal provision through which community health care became the responsibility of these member branches. This mandate became Senegal's national health policy. Thus, it was in accordance with the nation's health policy, as well as with principles of community health care formulated by Behrhorst, that in 1987 the citizens of Fatick formed their own health authority.

All facets of the community are represented in the membership of this health board, ranging from high school students to business persons, to housewives, to the head of the regional statistical service. The practical work of the board is done primarily through two subcommittees: a "mothers committee" which is responsible for provisions affecting the health of the community's families and children, and a "public health committee" responsible for undertaking broader health activities. There is also an executive committee which includes, along with the officers, the chairs of these two sub-committees and is responsible for coordinating and implementing public health programs, forming budgets, and establishing relations with outside health agencies. The members of the board are chosen by a general assembly consisting of representatives of the villages and districts in the region. They serve for two years and are eligible for reelection to a maximum of two additional terms. Regional physicians and trained health technicians are advisers to these board members, who make the decisions and take the actions.

The board as a whole meets two times a year and produces an operations report for the general assembly. The officers and chairs meet every month to discuss problems and the status of ongoing projects and to produce a financial report. The mothers committee and the public health committee meet regularly throughout the year, often with invited health officials, to plan and implement public health activities in the community. Financial support comes in part from the sale of "health care tickets" (approximately 50 cents for adults and 25 cents for children) which provide two days of health care at a local clinic. In addition, the Senegalese government contributes $38,000 annually to the program.

MEDICAL AND SOCIAL SUCCESSES

Two successful activities — one preventive and one medical — will illustrate the work of the Fatick community health board and its people-based strategies.

Cholera has been a highly prevalent disease in the region. Recently the board conceived and initiated a preventive program promoting increased hygiene. Using funds from the treasury, bottles of bleach were bought for every household. Health educators instructed all households to set up a basin of water containing a specified amount of bleach both in their eating area and next to the latrine. Household members were instructed to wash their hands with this diluted bleach before each meal and after each use of the latrine. In a community where there are high levels of hand contact during meals and also in public areas, especially in local markets, this simple prevention program has greatly decreased the spread of cholera in the community.

Cerebral malaria has also been a serious threat to the people of Fatick, especially to young children. An important activity undertaken by the health board was to make a prophylaxis for malaria (chloroquine) available for use with infants up to five years of age and with pregnant women. This program has resulted in important decreases in the incidence of cerebral malaria.

The impact of this malaria prevention campaign has proved remarkable not only from a medical standpoint but also from a social point of view. All human societies develop explanatory systems for disease, but traditional societies make much of social causes and treatments, especially for diseases that have a major social impact and inflict great suffering and death. These ideas and practices become part of the beliefs of the people, are transmitted down through the generations and are continually enriched with new elements.   They influence all aspects of daily life, including the most basic attitudes and behaviors.

In the case of cerebral malaria, the symptoms (including hallucination and raving) were so terrifying and mystifying that most people were unable to believe this disease could be caused by anything less than an attack by malevolent spirits or witches—especially when a community member previously in good health and spirits became subject to wild deliriums. The people of a rural African village are not inclined to take over-seriously the babbling of persons known to be chronically mentally ill, even if the things they say are accusatory in nature; but it is a quite different thing when such utterances come from someone who is sane. Should the afflicted person, perhaps a child, call out the name of a person in the community, that person is suspected of being a witch or a witch's double. The persons named and their families are then likely to be rejected and isolated by the community. Thus, as a byproduct of this disease, deep tensions and divisions have been produced and spread throughout the society.

The current decrease in the incidence of cerebral malaria in Fatick has reduced such social strife. While the form of medical control used here does not prevent all morbidity associated with ordinary malaria, it does prevent the neurologic complications. Thus, the people who instituted this program have been able to see for themselves that simply by introducing effective measures for malaria prevention they are able to eliminate neuro-behavioral aspects of malaria in an entire village.

This affords a fascinating example of how traditional people learn best and how their beliefs can become critically refined through experience in ways that do not destroy the community but rather strengthen it. The society develops not merely by adopting an outsider's medicine but through direct action and reflection of its own. Human relationships and the culture are maintained and even improved in the course of such change.

This process seems central to what Behrhorst meant when he spoke of the innovative power of the community approach in resolving community problems. It exemplifies a principle of primary health care which was advocated by Behrhorst and

A mothers committee at San Martín Jilotepeque in Guatemala.

enunciated at the Alma-Ata congress: Communities have the right and the authority to participate formatively and effectively in their own health care system. In our own case we found that as people began to participate they learned more quickly — which led in turn to their participating more fully.

During 1990 more than $120,000 was raised by the Fatick health board for its programs, including medical supplies, the maintenance of local health care facilities and outreach programs. Members of the board and the committees, knowledgeable about their own traditions and beliefs regarding disease and health, have been able to make the kind of decisions that involve and more fully benefit the community. While the people inhabit a very different clime and culture, they are following principles and objectives which came to expression in Chimaltenango.

References

Ministère de la Santé Publique, République du Sénégal
   1986, 1987, 1990 Statisques Sanitaires et Démographiques.
         Dakar, Sénégal: DRPF.
Bureau National du Recensement, République du Sénégal
   1988   Principaux Résultats Provisoires du Recensement Général de la
         Population et de l'Habitat du Sénégal (Mai-Juin). Direction de
         la Statistiques.
United States Agency for International Development
   1988   Unpublished statistics. Dakar, Senegal: Health, Nutrition and
         Population Office.
World Bank
   1990   World Development Report. New York: Oxford University
         Press.

On-farm experiment at Patzaj in Guatemala.

17

FEATURES OF EFFECTIVE AGRICULTURAL PROGRAMS IN GHANA AND OTHER LANDS

Wayne L. Haag

I will look back across the landscape of my 28 years in agricultural development and identify features of the "Behrhorst experience" that have proved most useful and that I now regard as essential. Most of my later experience has been gained through work with national agricultural research and production systems, which are responsible for the development and transfer of technology to small-scale, resource-poor farmers.

From 1973 to 1989 I worked as a plant breeder and agronomist with the International Center for Maize and Wheat Improvement (CIMMYT). Since 1990 I have been with the Sasakawa Global 2000 initiative, working in Ghana.[1] We cooperate with Ghanian re-

---

[1]The Sasakawa Global 2000 agricultural programs are jointly supported by the Sasakawa Peace Foundation and the Carter Presidential Center. Both Ryoichi Sasakawa and former president Jimmy Carter are actively involved. Noman Borlaug, president of the Sasakawa Africa Association, is a founder and senior consultant of these programs. After

searchers and extensionists to communicate production and post-harvest technologies to farmers: e.g., the use of new varieties, application of fertilizers, planting in rows, controlling weeds, building corn cribs, drying, cleaning and storing grains.

My career has taken me from Guatemala to residential work in Costa Rica, Mexico, Turkey, Egypt, Colombia and now Ghana. I have also served on a regional basis in India, Morocco, Syria, Portugal, Ecuador, Peru, Bolivia, Brazil, Uraguay, Paraguay and Argentina. I have made working visits to Pakistan, Hungary, Yugoslavia, Thailand, Japan, Honduras and Algeria. In all these places I have found striking similarities in what works and what does not. Both failures and successes reflect my learnings with Carroll Behrhorst in Chimaltenango during the early to middle 1960s. What we learned and practiced there at that time has become confirmed in the course of fighting the good fight in other lands.

LEARN WITH THE PEOPLE

I decided long ago that I would always try to contribute something concrete to the people with whom I cooperate and not simply give advice or place learned papers on the shelf. I would associate myself with organizations or agencies that pursue tangible results — that do not rest until improved practices and products actually reach farmers in their fields. If we set out to support a seed program, tons of quality seed must actually get to the fields in a timely way or we have not accomplished our purpose. If we are communicating a new post-harvest technology, this includes helping farmers actually build more suitable storage and drying structures. They and we must begin to see with our own eyes that there is less damage from molds, insects and rodents.

Once we are determined to contribute something concretely useful to people, it follows that we will respect those people and,

Behrhorst, I am obliged to name Norman Borlaug, a previous director of CIMMYT and winner of the Nobel Prize for his leadership of the "green revolution" in Asia, as a mentor.

as Behrhorst put it, "go to school with them." They will be our most obvious allies and they will be the judges as to whether we have been useful or not. Our own willingness to learn, and the self-confidence needed to learn, are perhaps the best legacies that we can leave with them.

In Chimaltenango our focus was on people-building rather than on building elaborate facilities — hence the major efforts to provide practical training, which was usually on-the-job training. Appropriate physical structures, equipment and supplies were, of course, necessary; but these co-evolved with the development of the people component. There was a harmony between the people being served and the "system" being developed to serve them.

In agriculture, the developing world is littered with hulks of buildings and farm machinery which proved inappropriate for the circumstances. The focus frequently has been on the highly visible, on erecting structures and placing equipment. Budgets have been consumed by these initial large investments, leaving little or no funding for program operation and maintenance, training, or public purchase of products.

An example can be found in the national seed industries of many countries. Huge investments have repeatedly been made to establish large-scale, modern, centralized seed-processing facilities. Most of these ventures have failed to supply quality seed to farmers for now obvious reasons. In Ghana, with support from USAID, the Ghana Seed Company built large processing and cold storage structures at five locations, which were designed and run by the government from top to bottom through a bureaucracy. These facilities proved too large for actual markets and for the less developed transportation infrastructure. The technology used was expensive and complex, imposing unaffordable overhead costs. As a result, the structures were grossly underutilized and were not maintained properly. Today empty buildings and silent refrigerators stand as monuments to a very familiar but very costly and inappropriate assumption.

The approach now being taken by more enlightened policy makers in Ghana, one which has also proven successful elsewhere (including Guatemala), is to decentralize and privatize commercial seed production. Our program was instrumental in achieving communication and joint action between the various parties and in procuring small amounts of initial credit for growers. The public now exercises a supportive role in the production of new seed varieties and in the extension of start-up loans and technical support to the new local commercial enterprises. These seed enterprises are closer to the farmers, vary in size, work in many places, and participate in educating farmers concerning the new varieties of quality seed. With the new private-public alliance, more good quality seed is being produced and sold than ever before. Our experience shows that even small, resource-poor farmers will lay out their hard-earned money for something that really works for them.

Nothing is more stifling than a system that obliges people to keep trying to adapt to it. We then spend year after year spinning our wheels. When development activities are people centered, we are compelled from the outset to identify appropriate, user-friendly methods and tools.

WORK WITH THE PEOPLE

Even at the prior level of identifying agricultural research priorities and developing new technologies, it is important to work closely with the farmers themselves. Certain technologies, to be sure, can be developed largely on experiment stations (for example, development of a new crop variety); but most technologies are best developed in the farmers' fields (for example, development of a recommended fertilizer practice). In all cases, early results must be tested extensively with farmers in their fields before they can be widely recommended and before they will be widely accepted.

I learned this early in Guatemala, where farmers were reluctant to invest their scarce resources in a technology previously untried by them. I therefore brought ten bags of fertilizers to the fields of ten farmers. We used one bagful in each of their fields and observed the difference, first during the growing stage and then at the harvest. We actually saw the connection between risk and benefit in practical terms—in plant color, size and yield, and also in terms of money in their pockets. The demonstration had been performed by the right persons in the right places and the critical impact had been achieved.

Something similar, on a much larger scale, can be said of the methods of CIMMYT with the Rockefeller Foundation and the Ford Foundation in promoting the "green revolution" in India and Pakistan. Something dramatic and closely allied with their own interests was needed to attract individual farmers—they became believers, by introducing a simple technology, they doubled or tripled their yields. The same kind of impact was needed in achieving understanding and support from the policy makers and politicians.

Learning by doing is the key. In the past, we agriculturalists put out small, specially groomed, picture-like demonstration plots and invited the farmers to come and observe them. This proved ineffective. Often little attention was paid to the costs involved or to the practicality of the recommended technology in real life circumstances. The farmers did not see these demonstrations as relevant to themselves. Today, the small demonstration conducted by the extension agent has finally given way to practical production plots run by the farmers themselves with the collaboration of technical staff.

On-farm research (OFR), though not yet universal, is now accepted by many national research systems. I have participated in the development of OFR systems in several countries and have found it revealing to observe the transformation that takes place not only in farmers but also in the research and extension personnel. When I came to Egypt in 1974, researchers were notably discouraged and despondent about their ability to impact the situation. They did not feel appreciated or useful. As technical experts, they were unwilling to allow that some of their recommendations might not be appropriate for farmers in this setting. Coming from academic and laboratory studies with little practical field experience, they were not tuned to social or bureaucratic problems affecting the farmers. They referred to farmers as ignorant and unwilling to accept innovations.

But I came to see those same formerly detached researchers, who were not very convinced of the relevancy of their work, become transformed into productive allies of the farmers once they joined the farmers in their fields. In conducting field trials with farmers the technical agent was obliged to learn about their circumstances, identify their priorities and make commitments to them. A respect and commitment grew up which had not existed before. Researchers left their defensive posture and became more self-confident and effective.

I wish to stress the point that development projects should be purposefully designed in such a way as to foster working relationships between those who provide services and those who are to make use of them.

EMPOWERMENT OF THE PEOPLE

Poor farmers often have low expectations with respect to the quantity and quality of their production. They assume that yields will simply depend on rainfall. Weevils and rodents are taken for granted. If these farmers are to take new initiatives, as Behrhorst repeatedly said, they must come to see that something more is actually within their reach and that it is subject to their own action.

Government itself can come to be viewed as a given, along with the rain and the rodents. Farmers have been led to believe that governments or agencies will deliver far more than they possibly can, or more than they actually will deliver for very long, especially where regimes are unstable. This has resulted in dangerous dependencies and a reduction of individual initiatives. Even food aid, while necessary for emergency disaster relief, can prove a disincentive to local production by destroying prices and the market. People become disempowered while they wait passively for food; they become empowered as they become producers of food and take up tasks of development that follow from that.

We have noted how in Ghana large scale centralized drying and storage structures were underutilized because of transport and other technical difficulties. Post-harvest losses continued. As a result of the recent efforts to secure grain quality on-farm, however, new possibilities have emerged. There is not only more efficiency in grain management but also increased independence and competency on the part of farmers. Farmers are able to hold their grains without losing them to insects and rodents—and also without losing them to temporary low prices in the market. Along the way, a nation's supply of food has become more secure.

Governments are prone to hold down prices in favor of a growing urban population, thereby victimizing farmers whose marketing cannot wait. But farmers are viewed in a different light once they become more productive and more capable of controlling their own produce. Governments begin to think of returns from strategic investment in farmers rather than of exploiting them. National economic development is seen as dependent on, not separate from, agricultural development.

INTEGRAL DEVELOPMENT

We have noted the separation which may exist between researchers, extensionists and farmers and the need to bridge this gap. A first step is to join the farmers in addressing their problems. This means going to work with them. While certain requirements must be met before larger projects can be initiated, there is usually something that can be done in the short term to improve an existing problematic situation. Behrhorst was one for getting on with the job. He did not wait for perfect conditions or until everything was in place—at which time interest may be lost.

In some programs the sequence of feasibility studies conducted prior to actually beginning the work seems interminable and proves self-defeating. There are plant breeders who are unwilling to introduce a new improved variety because they are waiting for their ideal specimen. This same expert reluctance preceded the introduction of the new grain varieties that catalyzed the "green revolution."

Behrhorst affirmed not only a need for beginning with what is available, but also a need for "integrated" rural development. Health considerations proved a key for bringing things together: agricultural productivity plus nutrition education, plus potable water supply and sanitation, plus availability of credit, cooperative land purchases and other elements that work together in a community setting to improve the people's health. My experience with the Chimaltenango program made me more sensitive to how my own specialties, plant research and agricultural practices, fit into and complement other aspects of rural development, especially with a view to health. I now see, for example, how quality protein maize (an enriched maize with double the normal levels of lysine and tryptophane in the protein) can make a valuable impact not only on yields but on nutrition. I now consider that, while the use of agrochemicals can be very important, we should be selective and careful in their use. I see how improvement in the post-harvest handling of crops can have desired effects not only on the farmer's purse but also on health, since many current health hazards are associated with crop deterioration. Thus, we should be aware of how our efforts enter into the larger picture. Specialized professional interests are not always identical with the interests of the people. In fact, separations between different development experts, specialties and projects can be very confusing to the people who are meant to be helped. Such barriers must be broken down along the way to integrating a whole set of complementary and mutually reinforcing possibilities.

DEALING WITH POLITICAL REALITIES

When I worked with the Chimaltenango program the social and political dynamics were complex and often dangerous. The path was not smooth. The very survival of the program later came into question. The future of the Chimaltenango program will depend on how wisely and constructively the new local leadership copes with continuing social-political realities. The Guatemalan experience holds unforgettable memories for people who now work in comparable situations elsewhere in the world.

People in agricultural development have learned that they cannot remain complacent with respect to government policies that affect pricing, credit, availability of inputs and other matters of vital importance to farmers. Some public policies have served as disincentives to producers. They have caused underinvestment in the rural sector by aiming to supply cheap food and other benefits to the urban sector at the farmer's expense. Involved farmers, who have gained confidence through an effective development program, will gradually create grass-roots pressures for influencing policies that affect agricultural production and development.

This need not mean, however, that public protest or partisan opposition are the appropriate strategies. We learned this with farmers in Turkey who experienced frequent changes in government, culminating in the military takeover of September, 1980. In Egypt we encountered intergroup tensions on religious and social grounds. Simple identification with one or the other of these contending parties could have weakened or even spelled the end of the program.

The appropriate course may lie less in making public protests than in attending to appropriate development activities within agriculture itself. We have noted how farmers became empowered in some places by means of local grain processing and holding facilities. Cotton farmers in Egypt, wheat farmers in India, and cocoa farmers in Ghana have all exerted pressures on the market by curtailing or withholding production. At the same time, public officials came to view agriculture, which was previously overlooked in favor of urban populations, as a critical factor in the development of their nations. The very success of small farmers caused these governments, which had previously followed a bureaucratic mega-building strategy of their own, to invest more strongly in the rural infrastructure.

It is important, in the course of seeking independence and empowerment, not to get side-tracked by extremist ideologies — for example, by partisan doctrines that all chemicals are dangerous, that anything artificial is unhealthy, or that every new crop variety disturbs the balance. Of course, we should all learn to use the resources at our disposal more judiciously and to practice better husbandry, but we should not in the process discard potentially valuable tools from our packet of alternatives. There are agricultural consultants who oppose the use of any purchased inputs by resource-poor farmers. They forget that some low cost alternatives are knowledge-intensive and might currently be further out of reach for poor farmers than the purchased inputs. For these farmers it may be necessary to introduce such technologies further down the road.

It is equally important that expatriate supporters and development workers do not themselves become entangled or bogged down in the local politics. This is sometimes hard to avoid, especially where vast inequities and their effects are manifest and our sympathies fall to one side on controversial issues. We may then be led, perhaps disastrously, to design a strategy for conflict in which the risks will be far more costly to locals than to visitors.

Poor people are parties with comparatively little power. A constant effort must be made, in view of the forces and trends arrayed against them, to avoid any simple "we versus they" mentality and to broaden the circle of program allies. If opposition must be taken, it should never be viewed as the end of the line. Some degree of acceptance must be gained from the established political power if the program is to survive and thrive.

It helps to remember that opponents do sometimes change their minds when they become more aware and if they are given the opportunity. It is also possible to exercise creativity in conceiving "win-win" strategies through which all parties can benefit, even where we first thought such possibilities did not exist. While technology in and of itself will not redress social ills, it is one of the very best allies in creating such win-win situations. In Ghana, revised storage facilities served to protect and empower farmers in the face of unfavorable pricing policies—and, at the same time, made farmers into allies of government for revised development policies. Similarly, societal conflicts over the role of women in agriculture have been helped toward resolution by the introduction of more amenable tools.

Genuine development, as Behrhorst insisted, takes time. It is wise to consider ways that could lead to an evolution of social contracts. For this, our moralist disposition may need to be tempered with a clearer sense of realities, and then directed so far as possible toward an agenda that enables progress while reducing conflict.

PROGRAM CONTINUITY

Programs belong to the people, not to supporters. It is the local people who must carry innovations into the future. Technical assistance founders when we do not remember this point. To be a skilled and energetic participant in development activities without taking over — that is the task, even though it is often easier said than done. This is one of the finer arts.

It is important, as we have seen, to design projects from the very outset in such a way as to place local people in leadership positions and place expatriates in clearly supportive roles. For the same reason, it is important to limit the number of expatriates involved with any project. They will then be required to develop closer working relationships with local staff. The local leaders and staff (who are sometimes inclined to trust foreign experts rather than one another) will then be required to cooperate with one another and thereby improve their management skills. Developing a clear set of responsibilities on all sides will go a long way toward encouraging accountability and building trust among all program staff, thereby assuring the program's continuity.

There is, finally, a question of continuity not only in program leadership but in program philosophy. More than one project has failed because the original rationale, which made it successful in the first place, was allowed to deteriorate or was drastically altered. As the winds of politics and opinion blow to and fro, the internal philosophical underpinnings of a successful program must be jealously protected and regularly communicated to participants.

It might seem that successful programs are the least likely to fall prey to political exploitation. The opposite is the case. A successful program is the most likely to be targeted and plundered. A contending political party or regime is often prone to condemn a program it does not fully understand, or to take over a successful program as its own. In either case the life of the program becomes threatened.

Lessons learned from the "Behrhorst experience" in Guatemala during the springtime of my life have become reinforced over the years in very different places. These learnings require us not to temper our courage but to augment it with judgment, not to diminish our convictions but to combine them with flexibility. They require us to sign up for the long haul, with no provision for quitting when the going gets tough. Because Behrhorst did this, his work goes on. The Chimaltenango program serves as a beacon to inspire, guide and reclaim us in many other parts of the world as we try to do our part.

18

FROM "HELPING THE VICTIMS" TO "BLAMING THE VICTIMS" TO ORGANIZING THE VICTIMS
Lessons from China, Chile and the Bronx

Victor W. Sidel

"HELPING THE VICTIMS"

It has come to be generally accepted that improvements in health over the past century—particularly the reduction of deaths early in life—have been the result of professional interventions to protect health and treat disease. If a health problem exists, this view holds, what is needed is the right professional to introduce the right technological solution that will protect the vulnerable from illness or heal the victims after they become sick.

In recent years, however, this model of reliance on professional solutions has come under a great deal of criticism. On the one hand, critics point out that professional medical models have been of limited use for what have become the leading causes of death in industrialized countries: heart disease, cancer, stroke and accidents. Nor have professional strategies in prevention or treatment had demonstrable success when applied to major causes of disability and despair, such as arthritis and other musculoskeletal disorders, mental illness, or abuse of alcohol and drugs.

Some critics have questioned the usefulness of the professional intervention model even in areas where it was assumed to have been most useful, in the prevention and treatment of infectious diseases. These critics suggest that the decrease in infectious diseases and a dramatic fall in death rates over the past century have been attributable, first, to the general rise in the standard of living in industrialized countries (improvement in food, shelter, clothing and other living conditions) and, secondarily, to improved public health techniques such as those for pure water and safe sewage disposal. They offer the judgment that most professional medical care techniques have had comparatively little impact on the improvement in life expectancy.

Concurrent with these criticisms has been concern, particularly in industrialized nations, over the enormous rise in the cost of professionalized medical care. As the percentage of older people in the population rises, as the complexity of medical procedures such as new imaging techniques and modern surgery increases, and as the number of highly trained people engaged in professional medical care expands, so does the cost of medical care to the society.

In the United States the medical care component of the consumer price index has risen 120 percent over the past decade—more than any other component. At present our national health expenditures amount to more than 13 percent of the gross national product (approximately $2,500 annually per person). The distribution of this vast amount of money is skewed, with almost fifty cents out of every dollar going to hospital and nursing home care and less than five cents of each dollar to health protection and health promotion. Moreover, the sources of payment for this enormous cost are unequally distributed and fall most burdensomely on the poor.

Perhaps most disturbing, however, are criticisms coming from the poorest countries of the world where even basic public health measures such as pure water supply, safe sewage disposal and most immunizations have yet to reach more than selected populations and where, despite some improvements, infant and child mortality rates, life expectancies and access to medical care remain far worse than in the rich countries. It was estimated in 1987 that the richest fifth of the world's population had annual public expenditures for health care averaging $600 per capita; the poorest fifth, $2 per capita. For the richest fifth, life expectancy at birth was 75 years; for the poorest fifth, 57 years. Among the richest fifth, the annual mortality rate for children under the age of five was 18 per 1,000; for the poorest fifth, 176 per 1,000. In poor countries fourteen million preventable deaths still occur annually among children less than five years old.

The training of highly professionalized personnel in poor areas or the setting up of "centers of excellence," usually with outside help and typically in cities, has had little general impact. Indeed, many people in poor countries suspect that professional interventions donated from the industrialized countries, even clearly useful ones like immunization or contraceptive devices, are designed more to serve the interests of people living in the donor countries than to help those living in the poor ones. Even where the giving appears to be truly altruistic or where the changes are made using internal resources, professional interventions seem painfully slow, ineffective or dysfunctional.

In short, both in poor countries and rich countries the "professional" or "help the victim" strategy (in which most of us have been educated and socialized) has come increasingly to be seen as limited and severely flawed. Moreover, in both poor and rich countries new models have been advocated to replace old ones. While these newer models differ from each other, they too share a tragic flaw: for they can lead on both sides to a net reduction, at least in the short-run, of health resources for those who need them.

General Economic Development

In many of the poor countries, the strategy has become one of general economic development or "modernization." Only general development, it is argued, can bring the improvement in living conditions that will help prevent illness and promote health. While this theory is an attractive one, recently industrialized societies — Mexico and Brazil are good examples in our hemisphere — have for the most part relied on "trickle-down" to reach the vast numbers of the desperately poor. Income distribution has changed little, if at all; the pie may now be larger but the poor still see very little of it. Health conditions of the poor remain disastrously inadequate compared to those of the relatively well-off individuals in their societies.

The conditions found in less developed countries are in some measure shared within industrialized countries, as may be seen, for example, in areas like the Bronx in New York City, where I work. Over a four-mile distance from the North Bronx to the South Bronx one witnesses an extraordinary increase in visible poverty. In the South Bronx the median income is less than half that in the North Bronx. Infant mortality rates in the South Bronx are 50 percent higher than those in the North Bronx; deaths attributed to drug dependence are five times as high and deaths from AIDS are twice as high. The incidence of measles, tuberculosis, venereal disease and lead poisoning are also much higher. Yet in the South Bronx, the area with the greatest deprivations, health care and medical services are actually being reduced through the disappearance of private offices, budget reductions for public programs and the closing of hospitals. In neither the United States nor in poor countries does general economic development trickle down sufficiently to make adequate health resources available to the have-nots.

"BLAMING THE VICTIMS"

In rich countries a strategy has emerged that is quite different from that of general development. This model focuses on the life-style of individuals as the major causes of poor health. Smokers are blamed for their lung cancer, alcoholics for their liver disease, drivers for their automobile accidents and hypertensives for their strokes.

Like the "general development" model in many poor countries, this "individual responsibility" model in rich societies offers a needed correction to that of complete dependence on "professionals"; yet it seems equally flawed. Many, if not most, unhealthy habits and lifestyles are culturally and economically influenced. Many of the current causes of ill health, such as environmental or occupational factors, are beyond the control of single individuals or families.

Indeed, health strategies which "blame the victim" appear at times to be a way of drawing attention away from societal causes of illness and of justifying the withholding of social resources from the prevention or care of illness. Such a strategy seems reflected, for example, in the requirement that every individual patient should pay a considerable amount out-of-pocket for each medical visit—so that pain in the personal pocketbook serves as a method for rationing scarce and expensive medical resources. (It is alleged that people do not understand how to use health services properly. If that is true, however, it is because community education has failed to help them understand.) Medical rationing by size of purse neglects the plain fact that persons who most need health resources are often those with the least ability to pay for them. Fashionable terms like "restraint" and "privatization" can serve as code words for victim blaming. Even a valuable phrase like "individual responsibility" can serve to take resources away from those who need them most.

Where then does that leave us? If the professional model, though certainly useful in some spheres, is flawed and inadequate to meet current human requirements, and if its replacements (general economic development in the poor countries and emphasis on individual lifestyles in the rich ones), while surely expressing important elements of health promotion, are also flawed and inadequate to meet current needs, what model will replace or complement them?

ORGANIZING THE VICTIMS

It was in the context of a search for new models that I came to know and admire the work of Carroll Behrhorst with communities in Guatemala. I learned of his work in Chimaltenango during the early 1970s while serving as a consultant to a joint study by UNICEF and the World Health Organization of "Alternative Approaches to Meeting Basic Health Needs in Developing Countries." Out of that study came the book entitled *Health by the People*, published in English, French and Spanish, for which Behrhorst wrote the chapter on the work in Guatemala. This book, together with the reports, described a new model, the "organizing" or "community" approach to health. Examples were to be found across entire societies such as China and Tanzania or as isolated efforts in countries such as Guatemala, India, Iran and Venezuela.

The organizing model gives special attention to people who have been socially and economically pressed into positions of underdevelopment, weakness and high risk. This is seen to be the case with entire societies, such as the postcolonial nations of Africa, and also within parts of broader societies, such as the inner cities and the Appalachian region of the United States. The response of this model to unhealthy conditions is community organization and collective action. Only by assuming power over their own lives and their own environments and by wielding that power to bring about substantial change can people make decisive and lasting improvements in their own health.

Lessons from China

During the twenty-five years from 1950 to 1975, the People's Republic of China (PRC) worked hard to develop an organizing model of health care. Near the end of this period, Ruth Sidel and I made repeated study visits to both rural and urban sites at the invitation of the Chinese Medical Association. In a country previously ravaged by starvation and communicable disease, one which possessed extremely limited personnel and facilities for modern medicine (and those concentrated in urban areas), significant and rapid change was achieved.

Following the establishment of the PRC in 1949, a National Health Congress in Peking had established four basic principles for health work: serving the peasants, workers and soldiers; putting prevention first; coordinating the practice of traditional Chinese and Western medicine; and integrating public health work with popular movements. As an example of the fourth principle, China fostered society-wide participation in health care and preventive medicine. Through "patriotic health campaigns," sanitation was improved and pests such as flies and mosquitos were considerably reduced. Opium use was brought to an end and venereal diseases were essentially eliminated through campaigns conducted by locally recruited and basically trained workers with community support. Vast numbers of people participated in similar campaigns against schistosomiasis and other parasitic infestations. Mobile health teams brought initial measures of preventive medicine to isolated areas.

During the Cultural Revolution of 1966-69 almost two million "barefoot doctors" were deployed (these were peasants working part-time as health workers who were trained to recognize and treat common diseases), along with three million trained rural health aides. Local cooperative medical care systems were developed and expanded in the rural areas. The economic bases for this development were the communes, into which the countryside was divided.

Health initiatives were undertaken at each level of rural organization. The smallest subdivision of a commune was the "production team" with a membership of 100 to 200 people. Members of a production team lived close to one another, usually in one or more small villages, and formed the basic social unit in the countryside. A cluster of teams, usually 10 to 20 teams, formed a "production brigade" and a typical commune was composed of 10 to 30 production brigades. The commune, usually comprising 30,000 to 50,000 people, was the lowest level of formal state organization in the rural areas and was analogous to neighborhoods in the cities. It was responsible for overall planning,

Health promoters in training at the Chimaltenango clinic in Guatemala for work in the villages and fields.

education, health and social services and for the operation of small factories that produced goods for its members as well as for trade.

Health care for the production teams was provided by barefoot doctors and, in some areas, by part-time volunteer health aides who worked under their supervision. The barefoot doctors fostered health care through health education, preventive medicine and the medical treatment of minor illnesses in their sparsely-equipped health stations. They also provided care in the fields, taking their medical bags with them while participating in agricultural work. The production teams chose health aides, whose primary role was to teach people about sanitation, collect night soil and ensure that it was adequately stored before being used as fertilizer. The health aides worked during their lunch hours or after their regular work and were not paid for this duty. Many large communes had their own hospital facilities to which patients were referred from the production brigade health stations.

Health care was provided in China's cities, as in the countryside, through activity at each organizational level. The smallest formal unit in the urban area was usually the "residents committee." Its health station, which served from 1,000 to 5,000 people, was near the homes of residents; its major functions were preventive — including health education and immunization, birth control, and the treatment of minor illnesses. Health workers at this level were local housewives, called "street doctors." The back-up institution for the health stations was the neighborhood "hospital" (which often had no beds and thus might more appropriately have been termed a clinic). These centers, which served as many as 50,000 people, were generally staffed by physicians fully trained in either traditional Chinese or Western medicine and by middle medical workers (nurses, technicians and assistant doctors).

Starting in the late 1970s, the new leadership of China shifted much of the emphasis in medical care (as in other aspects of China's work) toward "modernization" and technological change. Medical education was lengthened, specialty care was expanded and efforts to deprofessionalize medical care were abandoned. The elimination of the communes and of the residents' committees meant that the economic and social bases for local health work were largely destroyed.

Lessons from Chile

Efforts partly similar to those in China were made in Chile. In September 1970, Salvador Allende Gossens, a public health physician, won the presidential election of Chile as a candidate of the Unidad Popular, a coalition of political groups. He rapidly developed new social and economic policy in Chile, characterized by the nationalization of certain industries, redistribution of land from huge holdings to those who worked the land, changes in income patterns which favored poorly-paid workers, and reorienta- tion of production priorities toward the specific needs of poorer people.

In addition to the new economic policies there was a strong movement to revise and strengthen programs for health and human services. A basic objective was the "democratization" of the Servicio Nacional de Salud, the national health service of Chile. This was to be achieved by incorporating community organizations in health planning and decision making, eliminating excess bureaucracy, introducing new models of ambulatory care, and improving programs such as those for the prevention and treatment of alcoholism and those for milk distribution.

This policy, the incorporation of the community into health decision making processes, was officially stated in an August 1971 decree which directed the creation in every health center of a "local health council." This council was to include members elected by the local community organizations as well as represen- tatives of the local branch of the Colégio Medico (the Chilean medical association, to which all doctors were required to belong in order to practice medicine) and representatives of the health workers union which was composed of nonphysicians. The direc- tor of each health center was given the power to manage the personnel and budget of the center with the advice of the local health council.

During the three years of the Allende administration some 400 local health councils were established and community members began to asume a significant role in discussions of local health matters and decisions concerning the use of scarce health resources. The functions of the local health councils included the training of community volunteers for prevention of alcoholism and communicable disease and the creation of new satellite neighborhood health centers.

With the overthrow of the Popular Unity government in the 1973 military coup, many of these programs—and parts of the Servicio Nacional de Salud itself—were destroyed. A number of those who had worked to change health services were killed or driven into exile because their work was viewed as political. One of them, Roberto Belmar, escaped to the United States and worked with us in the Bronx.

Lessons from the Bronx

Roberto Belmar and others working in the Department of Social Medicine at Montefiore Medical Center attempted to adapt some of the lessons learned from China and Chile for health activities in the Bronx. A community health participation program was developed in the neighborhood that surrounds our medical center. The objective of this program was to develop a community based network that would encourage people to be concerned with their own health and that of their neighbors on a building-by-building and community basis. Within each apartment building interested volunteers were trained, not to serve as paramedics or as physician extenders, but to perform a very different role as health promoters for their buildings. The volunteers chose "health coordinators" as the name for their role.

The training of the health coordinators was conducted whenever possible at a site physically removed from the hospital itself. Because of this physical separation, community residents did not view the program as simply another extension of the hospital bureaucracy but rather as something separate and distinct, having a character all its own—smaller and on a more human scale than the hospital. On the other hand, the program's affiliation with the hospital permitted it to draw upon the hospital's resources for specific assistance when needed. For example, each health coordinator was given the name of a hospital staff member who could be consulted when a particular health problem was beyond the coordinator's competence.

Coordinators were recruited through existing neighborhood and tenant networks including block patrols, community organizations, individual acquaintances of functioning health coordinators, and in open workshops on health topics which were held for the public in the area. In their basic training program health coordinators considered the following topics: concepts of health, first aid, nutrition, relaxation and exercise, how to choose and use a doctor, how to make the health care system work for you and everyone else, interpersonal communications, community organizing, chronic diseases, the physical exam, addictions, child health, sex and family planning. Other more specialized training was provided when called for. While certain components were always included, the training program was designed in large measure by the participants. Volunteers in the program were asked what they wanted to learn or felt responsible to learn about health and health-related matters.

Trained health coordinators initiated several sorts of health activities in their apartment buildings. These included counseling individual tenants and families on matters of physical and mental health, referring neighbors to public agencies and community assistance programs when these were needed, helping neighbors with particular on-going health problems (including monitoring blood pressure of persons requesting it), giving first aid in emergencies, encouraging people to see a doctor when appropriate and accompanying them to the doctor or hospital when necessary, organizing cooperative buying, informing tenants of public programs and legislation affecting them directly, and organizing self-help groups and practical health workshops on questions ranging from how to stop smoking to methods of successful parenting.

As in China and Chile, when the national administration and political climate changed in the United states in 1981, this model program and its activities were sharply diminished. The federal government precipitously withdrew its modest support of these efforts and the limited funds that could be provided by the medical center and the community were insufficient to maintain the program.

WHAT IS TO BE DONE?

Our own efforts, as citizens and health professionals in the United States who have learned the importance of community approaches to health, will necessarily take place predominantly in our own communities. If we are to foster health in conjunction with community development, social justice and equity, I believe we must follow a number of basic principles.

First, we must respect the ancient medical dictum *primum non nocere*, "first, do no harm." We must do nothing to increase the powerlessness or the dependency of the community in which we live or serve.

Second, stating this point more positively, we must wherever possible strengthen determination, rechannel alienation and despair, and build the social structures that will enable people and communities to take responsibility for their health and destiny into their own hands. This includes fighting alongside them for retention of health resources in the community, including publicly supported services and their right to perform them. One of the ways in which we can do this is to transfer requisite knowledge and skills to members of the community.

Third, we must recognize, as we do this, that we have a primary task not only as teachers but as students, that of learning with the people how to produce effective social change and effective health care. The community then becomes a reference group for setting standards. The "diffusion of excellence" takes place from the bottom up rather than from the top down, from the community to the professional no less than the other way around.

Broader advocacies will also be needed. It seems clear from learnings both in this country and in other countries that understandings and policies must be pursued that secure stable and dependable public support of community-based initiatives in primary health care. Their survival should not be subject to shifts of administration or cyclical fiscal trends. Their work is cost effective in medical terms and has multiple benefits in the community.

Moreover, as we advocate and build such models in our own country, we should not forget the extent to which sickness in the poorer countries of the world is based on past and continuing expropriation of their local resources. The end of such exploitation and some restoration of resources, now being called for by the world's poor countries, are still strongly resisted through trade barriers, economic sanctions, political influence and even military measures. The level of foreign economic development aid in almost all rich countries (the Scandinavian countries and the Netherlands are notable exceptions) remains far below the .7 percent of gross national product advocated by the United Nations. While we seek stability for health practices in our own communities, we must also urge policies that ensure a rightful share of resources in poorer countries—those needed if they are to have self-empowering and healthy communities.

The "organizing" or "community" model will, of course, have to be introduced by the people themselves in every place, often in the face of strong and even brutal opposition. This does not mean that we in resource-rich areas can with justice stand idly by. As Carroll Behrhorst taught us, it is possible for health-committed persons to stand with and assist communities in poor areas as they organize community-based programs for health. Working within our own communities and supporting self-empowering initiatives on the part of people in other communities, we honor the memory and extend the work of one who helped to show us the way.

This paper is in part based on a W.K. Kellogg Foundation Lecture delivered at the 1979 annual conference of the Canadian Public Health Association and published in the *Canadian Journal of Public Health* 70:234-39.

19

TAKING CHARGE OF HEALTH
IN A CHICAGO NEIGHBORHOOD

John L. McKnight

Carroll Behrhorst made a profound impact on my thinking when I first met him in an international seminar at CIDOC (Centro Internacional de Documentación) in Cuernavaca, Mexico. We were collaborators in a series of extended consultations on health with Ivan Illich, prior to his writing *Medical Nemesis* (1976). These discussions greatly influenced all the participants. In Behrhorst's case, they served to confirm and clarify convictions which had come to characterize his work in Guatemala. In my case, Doc's contribution was critical, for he was the first medically trained person I had ever met whose primary focus was on "health" rather than "cure." As I later followed his work, I came to understand how this focus also determined his practice, which persistently and constructively referred to the most basic determinants of health.

While the CIDOC inquiries were attentive to issues of "development" in Latin American countries, their import was understood to extend to issues of health and medicine literally everywhere in the modern world. This essay describes how health understandings formed and clarified along with those of Behrhorst became flesh in a place very different from highland Guatemala—how Doc's influence was manifested in a North American city neighborhood which he did not visit until a decade later.

My story begins in the mid-1970s in a community of about 60,000 people on the west side of Chicago. The people of this neighborhood are poor and Black and many are dependent on welfare payments. They have formed a voluntary community organization which encompasses an area in which there were formerly two hospitals. One of these is now closed.

The neighborhood was previously all white. During the 1960s it went through a racial transition and, within a very few years, it became almost totally populated with Black people. The two hospitals continued to serve the white people who had previously lived in the neighborhood, leaving the Black people struggling to gain access to hospital services.

This became a local political struggle and the community organization finally "captured" the two hospitals. The hospitals were brought to accept neighborhood people, employed Black people on their staffs and treated patients from the neighborhood along with a diminishing number of white clients.

After several years, the community organization felt that it was time to stand back and look at the health status of their community. They found that, although they had gained access to the local hospitals, there was no evidence that the health of the people had improved significantly by virtue of those medical services.

The organization then called upon the Center for Urban Affairs. They asked us to assist them in finding out why, seeing the people had gained access to two hospitals, their health was not getting any better. We agreed to do a study of the medical records of these hospitals to see what brought people to receive medical care. We also took a sample of the emergency room medical records to determine the frequency of the various problems that brought the people into the hospitals.

We found that the seven most common reasons for hospitalization, in order of frequency, were:

1. Automobile accidents
2. Interpersonal attacks
3. Accidents (other than automobile)
4. Bronchial ailments
5. Alcoholism
6. Drug-related problems (medically and nonmedically administered drugs)
7. Dog bites

The people of the organization were startled by these findings. The language of medicine is focused on disease, yet the problems we identified had very little to do with disorders of an infectious or organic sort. The medicalization of health had led them to believe that the hospitals were appropriately addressing their health problems, but they discovered instead that the hospitals were dealing with many problems for which hospitals are always too late and which required treatment of another sort. It was an important step in the health consciousness of this community to recognize that modern medical systems are frequently dealing with maladies that are social problems rather than diseases. But social problems are the domain of citizens and their community organizations.

A STRATEGY FOR HEALTH

Having seen the list of maladies, the people considered what they should and could do about them. I wish to describe the first three decisions they made because each illustrates an important point.

First, as good political strategists, the people decided to tackle a problem which they felt they could solve. They did not want to take up a first battle and lose it. So they went down the list and picked dog bites, which caused about four percent of the emergency room visits at an average hospital cost at that time of $185.

How could this problem best be approached? It interested me to observe how the people in the organization conversed about this problem. The city government had employees who were paid to be "dog-catchers," but the organization did not choose to contact the city. Instead, they asked what they themselves could do to resolve the problem. They decided to take a small part of their money and use it for "dog-bounties." Through their block clubs they let it be known that for a period of one month, in an area of about a square mile, they would pay a bounty of five dollars for every stray dog that was brought in to the organization or had its location identified so that they could go and capture it.

There were packs of wild dogs in the neighborhood that had frightened many residents. The young of the neighborhood, on the other hand, thought that catching dogs was a wonderful idea, so they helped to identify them. In one month, 160 of these dogs were captured and cases of dog bites and resulting hospital visits decreased.

Two things happened as a result of this success. The people began to learn that their own action, rather than that of the hospital, determined their health. They were also building their organization by involving young people as community activists.

The second course of action was to deal with something more difficult—automobile accidents. "How can we do anything," the people asked, "if we don't understand where these accidents are taking place?" They wanted us to get information that would help them deal with the accident problem. But we found it extremely difficult to find information regarding when, where and how the accidents took place.

We considered going back to the hospitals and looking at the medical records to determine the nature of the accident that had brought each injured person to the hospital. If medicine were thought of as a system related to the possibilities of community action, this should have been possible. It was not. The medical records did not say, for example, "This person has a malady because she was hit by an automobile at six o'clock in the evening on January 3rd at the corner of Madison and Kedzie." Sometimes the records did not even document that the cause was an automobile accident. Instead, we would find simply that the person had a "broken tibia." It was a record system that obscured the community nature of the problem by focusing on the therapeutic to the exclusion of the primary cause.

We began, therefore, a search of the data systems of macroplanners. Finally we found one area planning group that collected data regarding auto accidents in the city. This data was collected in a complex computerized system used in large-scale planning to facilitate automobile traffic! We persuaded the planners to do a printout that could be used by neighborhood people for their own action purposes. It had never occurred to the planners that such use could be made of their information.

The printouts were so complex, however, that the organization could not comprehend them. So we took the numbers and transposed them onto a neighborhood map showing where accidents took place. Where people were injured, we put a blue X. Where people were killed, we put a red X. We did this for all accidents during a period of three months.

In that neighborhood area of 60,000 residents, during this three-month period, there occurred more than 1,000 accidents. On the map the people could see, for example, that during this period six people had been injured and one person had been killed in a single area 60 feet wide. They immediately identified this place as the entrance to a parking lot for a department store. Armed with this information that had been "liberated" from its medical and macroplanning captivity, the citizens were now ready to act (rather than be treated) by dealing with the store owner.

The experience with the map had two consequences. First, it provided an opportunity to invent ways of dealing with a health problem that the community could understand—it allowed the community organization to negotiate with the department store owner and force a change with respect to the parking lot entrance. Second, it became very clear that there were accident problems that the community organization could not handle directly. For example, one of the main reasons for the accidents was that distant authorities had decided to make several of the streets through the neighborhood into major throughways for automobiles going from the heart of the city out to the suburbs. Those who made this trip were a primary cause of injury to local people. Since dealing with this problem was not within the control of people at the neighborhood level, they now understood the necessity of getting other community organizations involved in a similar process. Together they could, perhaps, assemble enough power to move the authorities to change the policies that served only the interests of those who lived outside the city and used the neighborhoods as their freeway.

A third community action developed when the people focused on "bronchial problems." They learned that nutrition was a factor in these problems and concluded that the people in their neighborhood did not eat enough fresh fruit and vegetables. In the city, particularly in the winter, these foods were very expensive. Could they grow fresh fruit and vegetables themselves, as many had done in previous settings? This seemed difficult in the heart of the city. Then several people pointed out that most of their dwellings were two-story apartment buildings with flat roofs. They proposed building greenhouses on the rooftops to grow their own fruits and vegetables. So they built one greenhouse as an experiment. Then, a number of fascinating things began to happen.

Initially, the greenhouse had been built to deal with a health problem — inadequate nutrition. The greenhouse was a tool, appropriate to the environment, which people could build and use to improve their health. Soon, however, people began to see that the greenhouse was also an economic development tool. It increased their income since it produced commodities that could also be offered for sale.

Soon another use for the greenhouse appeared. In Northern cities, energy costs are very high and are a great burden for poor people. One of the main places where people lose or waste energy is from the rooftops of their houses — but placing a greenhouse on top of the roof converted this energy loss into an asset. The energy that escaped from the house went into the greenhouse where heat was needed. The greenhouse was, therefore, a way of putting energy to use that would otherwise have gone to waste.

Yet another use for the greenhouse developed by chance. The community organization owned a retirement home for elderly people. One day an elderly member discovered the greenhouse. She went to work there, and told others about it. They started coming to the greenhouse every day to help care for the plants. The administrator of the retirement home noticed that the attitude of these residents had changed. They were excited. They had found a function and a purpose. The greenhouse had become a tool to empower the elderly — it enabled discarded people to become productive.

MULTILITY VERSUS UNITILITY

Though they might not have put it this way, the people in this Chicago neighborhood had begun to learn something about technology. Here was a simple tool — a greenhouse. It could be built and used locally, and its "outputs" included health, economic development, energy conservation and productive activity for older people. A simple tool requiring minimum "inputs" produced multiple "outputs" with few negative side effects. We called this kind of tool a "multility."

Most tools in a modernized consumer-oriented society are the reverse of this. They are systems requiring a complex organization with multiple inputs that produce only a single output. Let me give an example. The United States imports bauxite from Jamaica, copper from Chile, rubber from Indonesia, oil from Saudi Arabia and lumber from Canada, which requires the use of labor in all these countries. These resources are then processed by a corporation, using additional labor and professional skills, to manufacture and market a single commodity — for example, the electric toothbrush. Such a tool we now call a "unitility." It has multiple inputs and one output. If tools are, by definition, labor-saving devices, then this is really an anti-tool. If you add up all the labor that goes into producing it, the sum is vastly larger than the labor that is saved by its use.

The electric toothbrush and the system for its production exemplify a technological mistake. The greenhouse exemplifies a technological possibility. A unitility disables local capacities and maximizes exploitation. A multility minimizes exploitation and enables community action.

Similarly, a hospitalized focus on health disables community capacities by concentrating on therapeutic tools and techniques requiring tremendous inputs, but having limited outputs in terms of standard health measures. Needed are health tools that create citizen action and actually improve health.

CONCLUSIONS

Let me draw several conclusions from the community health work that we have described.

First, it is important to note that this health action process strengthened a community organization. Converting medical problems into community issues proved central to health improvement. Therefore, since the action increased the organization's vitality and power, it initiated a critically important health development. Effective health action will lead away from overdependence on professional tools and techniques toward community building and citizen action.

Second, effective health action identifies what can be done at the local level with local resources. It also identifies those external assumptions, authorities and structures that place limits on the ability of the community to act in the interest of its health.

Third, health action develops tools for the people's use that are within their own control. Developing such tools may require and justify some diminution of the resources consumed by the medical system. As community health activity becomes more effective, the swollen balloon of medicine should expand less slowly.

For example, after the dogs were captured through neighborhood initiative, the hospital lost clients. While we cannot expect the medical system to reduce its claims for resources and power, community action has made clear the limitations and inadequacies of medicalized definitions of health and health care. Poor people need income. They do not want to trade in an economy where they simply exchange their work for more therapy. They could use some of the resources medicine now claims for its therapeutic purposes to diminish their therapeutic need. At present, in Illinois, one percent of Medicaid expenditures equals three times the amount of all grants to community organizations and their health promoting activities.

These three principles of community health action suggest that improved health will require moving away from simply being "medical consumers." If we may generalize from the experience here described, one sickness we all face is the captivity of tools, resources, power and consciousness by medical "unitilities" that produce consumers rather than actors.

Health is a social and political question. It requires action by citizens and communities. The health action process can facilitate a next "health development" by translating medically defined problems and resources into actionable community problems.

This Chicago west side community has continued its struggle with questions of health. During the years that followed these events, the medical system and its allied health planners have further abandoned the neighborhood. To fill the vacuum, an alliance of neighborhood organizations has now constituted itself the "West Side Health Authority." This self-designated local civic authority has developed an agenda of its own with respect to medical facilities and professionals in the area, seeking to shape them in terms of its own priorities and concerns. A second emphasis has been placed on developing the capacity of local citizens to communicate health through their common actions as experienced and caring neighbors. When Carroll Behrhorst visited this Chicago neighborhood in 1986 there was, not surprisingly, a remarkable meeting of minds. This popular ascendance of local citizens to control over the definition and promotion of health in their community is a living memorial to the wider importance of Doc's vision and practice.

The story of this community was previously presented by John McKnight in a gathering of international health workers convened by the Dag Hammarskjöld Foundation in Uppsala, Sweden, and was published in the journal of the foundation, *Development Dialogue* (1978:1).

Woman with kids on a farm at Las Mercedes in Guatemala.
"We borrowed and fed the mother, hoping for a good milking
goat. What did we get but two little male goats." Males have
"unitility," not much "multility."

20

AN INVITATION FROM CHIMALTENANGO

Carlos Xoquic
Interview and translation by John Puelle

I have been with the Behrhorst program almost from its beginning in 1962. I was one of the original health promoters, and served for many years as a coordinator of their work. Now I have become president of the Fundación Guatemalteca para el Desarrollo "Carroll Behrhorst."

What has kept me engaged in this way for thirty years? A short answer is that I continue because I like the program. The philosophy here has always been one of love, humanism and unconditional service—that is, service with people on their terms for as long as they find it important. This is what keeps me and my people involved.

A longer answer is that Carroll Behrhorst had a special way of working. We Guatemalans were glad to work along with him.

Carlos Xoquic as coordinator of health promoters. He is now president of the Fundación Guatemalteca para el Desarrollo "Carroll Behrhorst."

Now that he is gone, we are determined to continue on the same path and work with one another in the same way.

The program does not belong to me. The role of a board president is, after all, a passing thing. The people with whom we work are the owners of the program. The inheritance which the doctor left belongs to them. We want to perpetuate that as best we can.

We have achieved many objectives over the past 30 years. We have done a lot to raise the rural people in the highlands—which is to say they have done a lot to raise themselves. In spite of conflict and setbacks, we have realized the goal of creating and protecting an institution that works with the people on the people's terms. The key continues to be one of sensitizing our staff and our communities to the notion of such unconditional service.

Looking back, we can see how far we have come. As signs of this, the sons of two original health promoters, Seferino González and Fidel Sacbajá, have graduated from medical school. Leonel Sacbajá is now one of our staff physicians here at the foundation. The son of another health promoter, Santiago Tuctuc, will soon graduate from seminary and return as a priest. But the rising awareness and development of many people in the highlands is the major proof of the worth of our program.

The partnership agreement which governs the relationship between the Guatemalan Foundation and the Behrhorst Clinic Foundation in the United States is entering a new phase. The North American group is now even more dynamic in spreading the word and raising funds than it was years ago. To that foundation I commend the readers of this book who want to know more about us and our work.

For our part, we Guatemalans must never make the mistake of considering a donor or sponsor as a father who is there to take care of his children. Over the years we have learned a lot about being equal partners, so that there can be gains on both sides. Neither we nor the North Americans can achieve our desires and dreams if we do not work together. There is a lot to do by way of safeguarding this relationship; that is why I accepted the chairmanship of the local board.

One example of how this cooperation can work comes from my own home town of Sumpango. I am a member of the school committee there. Through a long process of working with the community, of listening and learning from mutual feedback, we have built a new school. We did this together. This kind of process is basic to the Behrhorst program.

Finally, I wish to say to readers of Behrhorst's written words and the words of others who have worked with us along the way, that there are also ways for you to work with us. But North Americans should first come to know our program here to change their way of thinking. There is no better way to do this than by visiting and becoming sensitive to the way we do things in Chimaltenango. It is through practical experience that we learn to become partners and walk the same path.

BIBLIOGRAPHY AND RESOURCES

Regardless of specific objectives, the basic "development" strategy must be empowerment of the people, particularly the poor. It would seem futile to continue outreach programs and service schemes if their guiding policy is not this. There will be more poor and more sick by the year 2000 (not "health for all") if the process of initiative and power are not clearly noted and addressed.

— Carroll Behrhorst,
The Chimaltenango Development Program
(1982 Draft)

Probably no two institutions have deposited themselves on others with such zeal as have the church and medicine. It is undeniable that this depositing has had its uses, but the price has also been high. Negative dependencies have resulted that have flawed initiative, self-reliance and independence. Though I must add with haste and emphasis that various groups of Lutherans and other denominations have continued to support this program in its integrity down to the present day. Moreover, one-way missions are being reversed or are now going both ways.

— The Chimaltenango Development Program
(1982 Draft)

Professional and biomedical advances have failed to reach, and show little promise of reaching, many large populations about the globe. To help fill this vacuum, community people are the great untapped resource. This untapped resource, if mobilized and supported, will contribute significantly to what now seem scarce resources for health and development. It will assure that the people's felt and expressed needs are addressed. It will serve as a catalyst in solving a wide variety of community problems bearing on health. It will stop runaway costs which now also threaten developed societies. It possesses great intrinsic value for the participants, creating responsibility, self-determination and cooperation. It is healthy.

— E. H. Christopherson Award Lecture (1988)

THE CHIMALTENANGO DEVELOPMENT PROGRAM

Following are selected titles of monographs, addresses, periodic literature and audio-visuals produced by Carroll Behrhorst and the foundations in Guatemala and the United States. Also included are materials by others who specifically treated the Chimaltenango Development Program or prepared manuals for its work. Most items are available through the Behrhorst Clinic Foundation, Inc., P.O. Box 1815, New York, NY 10009.

PRIMARY WRITINGS AND ADDRESSES OF CARROLL BEHRHORST

Original papers and correspondence are preserved in the Henry and Catherine Behrhorst Memorial Collection of the Howard-Tilton Memorial Library at Tulane University.

1960   Medical Project for Guatemala. For the Guatemalan Council, Lutheran Church — Missouri Synod, with resulting resolutions.

       Medical Mission in Latin America. With resolutions passed by the Caribbean Conference.

1961   Observations about the Administration of Mission Work with Special Reference to the Medical Programs of the Church.

1970   Address to the Student Body of St. John's College (Winfield, Kansas).

1971   Proposal for a youth study center with the Kaqchikel people in La Bola de Oro.

1972   Report on a Survey Trip through Africa and Asia. For the Director of Health Affairs, Commission on Ecumenical Missions and Relations, United Presbyterian Church U.S.A.

1973   Thoughts on Alternatives in Community Health. For consultations at Centro Intercultural de Documentación in Cuernavaca, Morelos, Mexico.

1974 Articles in Voz del Pueblo: Mensuario Cultural al Servicio de las Comunidades en Desarrollo. San Juan Comalapa, Chimaltenango. Shortness of breath, vomiting, fever, and other diseases along with problems of agriculture and small animal husbandry.

1974 Report on a Visit to Methodist Work in Haiti. For Methodist Medical Missions.

1975 Report on a Trip to Papua, New Guinea. For the Churches Medical Council of Papua, New Guinea.

1976 Alternative Approaches to Primary Health Care in Rural, Medically Deprived Areas. Address to the Texas Rural Health Conference.

Proposal for Integrating Health Promoters from the Behrhorst Program with those of the Guatemalan Ministry of Public Health and Social Assistance.

Community Inclusion of the Disabled. Address in Oxford, England, to a Symposium on Appropriate Technology and Delivery of Health and Welfare Services for the Disabled in Developing Countries.

1977 Health to the People. Address to the American Medical Students Association. The New Physician, Spring:32-34.

Rethinking Health Care: A Search for Complementary Paradigms relating Consumer Competence for Self Care and Physician Expertise. Presentation to a symposium sponsored by Project REACH.

Small Stories about Health. Prepared for a consultation with members of the U.S. Congress.

1978 Introduction and Design for Expansion of the Chimaltenango Development Program in Uspantán, Quiché, Guatemala. Recent Happenings in Uspantán, Quiché, Guatemala.

1981 The Conflicts in Chimaltenango, Guatemala, as they relate to the Foundation.

1983 A Brief Policy Statement of the Chimaltenango Development Program.

1983 The Chimaltenango Development Program, Guatemala. Previously described in: Contact 19 (Geneva: Christian Medical Commission, World Council of Churches), February, 1974, and Environmental Child Health, December, 1974. Expanded in: Kenneth Newell, ed., Health by the People. Pp. 30-56. Geneva: World Health Organization, 1975. Summarized in guest editorial for Club of KOS for Health Care newsletter, June, 1978. Revised in: Ulli Steltzer, Health in the Guatemalan Highlands. Pp. xi-xxxv. Seattle: University of Washington Press, 1983.

1986 Report to Former Medical Students. After the violence of the early 1980s.

1987 Report of visits with previous collaborators in Europe.

1988 E.H. Christopherson Award Lecture. To the American Academy of Pediatrics annual meeting in San Francisco.

1989 Lecture notes on primary health care to international students at Tulane University School of Public Health and Tropical Medicine.

Vision of the Fundación Guatemalteca para el Desarrollo "Carroll Behrhorst" with Recommendations for the Near Future.

BOOKS DESCRIBING THE CHIMALTENANGO PROGRAM

Barton, Edwin
1970 Physician to the Mayas: The Story of Carroll Behrhorst. Philadelphia: Fortress Press.

Heggenhougen, H. K.
  1977 Health Care for the "Edge of the World" — Indian Campesinos
        as Health Workers in Chimaltenango, Guatemala: A Discussion
        of the Behrhorst Program. Ph.D. dissertation to New School for
        Social Research, New York City. University Microfilms Inter-
        national, P.O. Box 1764, Ann Arbor MI 48106.
Muller, Frederik
  1979 Participación Popular en Programas de Atención Sanitaria
        Primaria en América Latina. Pp. 124-35. Medellín: Universidad
        de Antioquia.
Newell, Kenneth (ed.)
  1975 Health By the People: In Search of a New Medicine. Pp. 30-56.
        Published in English, Spanish, German and French. Geneva:
        World Health Organization.
Steltzer, Ulli
  1983 Health in the Guatemalan Highlands. Seattle: University of
        Washington Press.

AUDIOVISUALS

  1976 Seeds of Health. Film by Peter Krieg. Produced by World
        Council of Churches and Teldok Films. Script advice by
        Christian Medical Commission of the World Council of
        Churches and World Health Organization. Available with
        English, French, German and Spanish sound tracks.
  1976 Surviving the Trembling Earth. Film in English and Spanish by
        Ralph Kruse. Also 1,000 slides and audio script by Richard
        Burd. Available from Communications Services, Governors
        State University, University Park, IL 60466.
  1977 Carroll Behrhorst: Doctor to the Maya. Film by John Hagar.
  1984 Hope in the Highlands. Script and slides produced by the
        Behrhorst Clinic Foundation, Inc. Also scripted for children.
  1985 Conversations with Dr. Behrhorst. VHS video by Page
        Burkholder.
  1990 Paso a Paso: Step by Step toward the Future in Chimaltenango.
        VHS video by Page Burkholder.

PROGRAM REPORTS AND RESOURCES OF THE BEHRHORST CLINIC FOUNDATION

Behrhorst Clinic Foundation
  1976 The Behrhorst Clinic Program as it was before the Earthquake
        of 1976.
Horton, Jonathan C.
  1986 Medical Guide to the Behrhorst Foundation Hospital. Prepared
        for the Guatemalan Block in Community Medicine, A Program
        Coordinated by the Roger Thayer Stone Center for Latin
        American Studies at Tulane University.
Knebel, Fletcher
  1976 The Man and His Ideas.
Knebel, Fletcher and Patricia Krause (eds.)
  1974 Behrhorst Clinic Foundation newsletters.
Margoluis, Richard
  1991 Evaluation of and Recommendations for the Behrhorst/Nuevo
        Amanecer Health Promoter Program of Chimaltenango, Guate-
        mala.
Monzón, Roderico and Richard Margoluis
  1991 Master Work Plan of the "Carroll Behrhorst" Guatemalen
        Development Foundation to begin in 1992.
O'Connor, Patricia
  1986 Special Report on the Behrhorst Foundation of Chimaltenango,
        Guatemala.
O'Connor, Patricia, Robert R. Franklin, and Carroll Behrhorst
  1987 Hospital Record Studies as a Tool for Staff Education: A
        Participatory Research Project in Guatemala. Journal of
        Community Health 12(2-3):92-107.
Ward, Victoria and Angelika Bauer
  1984 ¿Quién Guarda la Salud? A people's manual on the uses of
        local herbs for health. Guatemala: Litorama Press.

EVALUATION AND CRITICISM

Bent, Muriel F.
  1978 The Role of Auxiliary Health Workers in the Delivery of
        Primary Health Care. Ottawa: International Development
        Research Centre.
Brockhoff, Dorothy
  1971 Physician to the Mayas. Washington University Magazine
        (Spring).
  1974 The House Across the Road. Option (January 7).
Bunch, Roland
  1970-71 Progress Report Nos. 6 and 7: Chimaltenango Development
           Program. Oklahoma City: World Neighbors.
Council for Christian Medical Work
  1976 Rebuilding Lives in Guatemala. Cross and Caduceus 25(1):2-3.
Crawshaw, Ralph
  1986 Letter from Guatemala. The Club of KOS for Health Care 9(2).
Edelen, John S.
  1966 A Descriptive Study of the Behrhorst Hospital. New York:
        College of Physicians and Surgeons, Columbia University.
Ekstrom, Dale
  1988 A Lesson in Compassion. The New Physician, September:43-44.
Glittenberg, JoAnn
  1974 Adapting Health Care to a Cultural Setting. American Journal
        of Nursing 74(12):2218-2221.
  1988 The Behrhorst Program: A Model for Primary Health Care.
        Journal of Professional Nursing 4(6):400,459.
Greenwood, A.
  1972 Paramedical Workers in Action: A Report of the Behrhorst
        Clinic in Guatemala. Oklahoma City: World Neighbors.
Griffin, Katherine
  1986 Clinic's Pioneering Outreach Program Faces Shaky Future.
        American Medical News (December 12).
Habicht, John-Pierre
  1973 Delivery of Primary Care by Medical Auxiliaries: Techniques of
        Use and Analysis of Benefits Achieved in Some Rural Villages
        in Guatemala. Plus critical follow-up discussion with officials
        and senior advisors of the Pan American Health Organization.
        In: Medical Care Auxiliaries. PAHO, World Health
        Organization Scientific Publications 278:24-39.

Horton, Jonathan C.
1987 The Behrhorst Foundation after Twenty-Five Years: A Report from Chimaltenango, Guatemala. New England Journal of Medicine 316(June 25):1666-1669.
Kingma, Stuart J.
1978 The Chimaltenango Development Programme and the Behrhorst Clinic. Report of a visit by a staff member of the World Health Organization, Geneva, Switzerland.
Lind, Kristin and Sven Björklund
1970 It is their Silence that Hurts. Transcription of talks by Dr. Carroll Behrhorst in a highland village and on hospital rounds with health promoters. Prepared for Swedish radio and television.
Marty, Micah
1987 New Medicine and Ancient Traditions in the Land of the Maya. Second Opinion 4:92-121.
Morgan, Edward P.
1976-1980 In the Public Interest, ABC News, Washington, D.C. Commentary no. 105 treats responses after the earth-quake; nos. 445, 446, 540 treat responses during the violence.
Murphy, C. Michael
1966 Analysis of Rural Empirical Practitioners. Lexington: University of Kentucky College of Medicine.
Paddock, William and Elizabeth
1973 We Don't Know How—An Independent Audit of what they call Success in Foreign Assistance. Includes criticism of the Behrhorst foundation and the health promoters for independence from government medical programs. Ames: Iowa State University Press.
Smith, Sandy
1992 Mission to Chimaltenango. Criticizes some medical practices and communications with government during the violence. Attached are interviews by Susan G. Parker with Hortensia Otzoy de Cap and John Puelle concerning old principles and new leadership at the foundation. The New Physician, April:17-21.

Westreich, Larry
  1990 Modern Medical Training Confronts Guatemalan Poverty. A
        medical student expresses, along with appreciations, some
        frustrations over lack of medicines and equipment. Minnesota
        Medicine 73(January):19-22.

NEWSPAPER FEATURES, BULLETINS, BROADCASTS

A list of news articles, radio and TV commentaries and other public
communications is available through the office of the Behrhorst Clinic
Foundation, Inc.

CULTURE AND HEALTH IN GUATEMALA

Michael H. Logan and Robert Patrick

The following titles, mostly in English, have been selected to help interested readers find printed information on the peoples of Guatemala, with a particular emphasis on the Maya. The list is not intended to be comprehensive or exhaustive. Specific sources on the Behrhorst program cited above, and on primary health care policies cited below, are not repeated.

Adams, Richard N.
   1952 Un Análisis de las Creencias y Prácticas Médicas en un Pueblo Indígena de Guatemala. Publicaciones Especiales del Instituto Indigenista Nacional (Guatemala) 17:1-105.
   1955 A Nutritional Research Program in Guatemala. In: Health, Culture, and Community, B. Paul (ed.). Pp. 435-458. New York: Russell Sage Foundation.
   1957 Cultural Surveys of Panama, Nicaragua, Guatemala, El Salvador, Honduras. Washington, D.C.: Pan American Sanitary Bureau, Scientific Publication 33.
   1970 Crucifixion by Power. Austin: University of Texas Press.
Adams, Richard N. (ed.)
   1972 Community Culture and National Change. Middle American Research Institute, Publication 24. New Orleans: Tulane University Press.
Adams, Richard N. and Arthur J. Rubel
   1967 Sickness and Social Relations. In: Handbook of Middle American Indians, vol. 6. M. Nash (vol. ed.) Pp. 333-355. R. Wauchope (general ed.). Austin: University of Texas Press.
Anderson, John E., et al.
   1981 Determinants of Fertility in Guatemala. Journal of Social Biology 20:77-86.
Anderson, Marilyn
   1978 Guatemalan Textiles Today. New York: Watson-Guptil.
Annis, Sheldon
   1981 Physical Access and Utilization of Health Services in Rural Guatemala. Social Science and Medicine (Medical Geography) 15D:515-523.

1987   God and Production in an Indian Town. Austin: University of
       Texas Press.
Asturias, Miguel Ángel
1974   Hombres de Maíz. Editorial Universitaria Centro-americana,
       Educa.
Balderson, Judith B.
1981   Malnourished Children of the Rural Poor: The Web of Food,
       Health, Education, Fertility, and Agricultural Production.
       Boston: Auburn House.
Barry, Tom
1986   Guatemala: The Politics of Counterinsurgency. Albuquerque:
       The Resource Center
Bates, F., Farrel, T. and J. Glittenberg
1984   The 1976 Guatemalan Earthquake Study: Its Findings and
       Implications. Vol. 5. Athens: University of Georgia Press.
Blaco, Ricardo A.
1974   Height, Weight, and Lines of Arrested Growth in Young
       Guatemalan Children.   American Journal of Physical
       Anthropology 40:48-59.
Bogin, Barry, et al.
1989   Longitudinal Growth in Height, Weight, and Bone Age of
       Guatemalan Ladino and Indian School Children. American
       Journal of Human Biology 1:103-113.
Bogin, Barry and Robert B. MacVean
1984   Growth Status of Non-Agrarian, Semi-Urban Living Indians in
       Guatemala. Human Biology 56:527-538.
Bossert, T., et al.
1987   Sustainability of U.S. Government Supported Health Projects in
       Guatemala.   Washington D. C.:   Agency for International
       Development.
Brintnall, Douglas
1979   Revolt Against the Dead: The Modernization of a Mayan
       Community in the Highlands of Guatemala.   New York:
       Gordon and Breach.
1980   Model of Changing Group Relations in the Maya Highlands of
       Guatemala. Journal of Anthropological Research 36:294-315.
Bunzel, Ruth
1959   Chichicastenango: A Guatemalan Village. Seattle: University of
       Washington Press.

Burleigh, E., C. Dardano, and J. R. Cruz
   1990 Colors, Humors, and Evil Eye: Indigenous Classification and Treatment of Childhood Diarrhea in Highland Guatemala. Medical Anthropology 12(4):419-441.
Caceres, Armando, et al.
   1991 Plants Used in Guatemala for the Treatment of Respiratory Diseases. 1. Screening of 68 Plants Against Gram-Positive Bacteria. Journal of Ethnopharmacology 31:193-208.
Canby, Peter
   1992 The Heart of the Sky: Travels Among the Maya. New York: Harper-Collins.
Carmack, Robert M.
   1973 Quichean Civilization. Berkeley: University of California Press.
   1981 The Quiché Mayas of Utatlán: The Evolution of a Highland Guatemalan Kingdom. Norman: University of Oklahoma Press.
Carmack, Robert M. (ed.)
   1988 Harvest of Violence: The Maya Indians and the Guatemalan Crisis. Norman: University of Oklahoma Press.
Carmack, Robert M., John Early, and Christopher Lutz (eds.)
   1982 The Historical Demography of Guatemala.   Albany, N.Y.: Institute for Mesoamerican Studies, SUNY-Albany.
Carter, William E.
   1969 New Lands and Old Traditions: Kekchi Cultivators in the Guatemalan Lowlands. Gainsville: University of Florida Press.
Clay, Jason (ed.)
   1983 Voices of the Survivors: The Massacre at Finca San Francisco, Guatemala. Cultural Survival 10:1-106.
Colby, Benjamin N. and Pierre van den Berghe
   1969 Ixil Country: A Plural Society in Highland Guatemala. Berkeley: University of California Press.
Colby, Benjamin, and Lore M. Colby
   1981 The Daykeeper: The Life and Discourse of an Ixil Diviner. Cambridge: Harvard University Press.
Cosminsky, Sheila
   1975 The Evil Eye in a Guatemalan Community. In: The Evil Eye, C. Maloney (ed.). New York: Columbia University Press.
   1977a Alimento and Fresco: Nutritional Concepts and their Implications for Health Care. Human Organization 36(2):203-207.
   1977b Childbirth and Midwifery on a Guatemalan Finca. Medical Anthropology 1(3):69-104.

1982 Childbirth and Change: A Guatemalan Study. In The Ethnography of Reproduction and Fertility, C. MacCormack. Pp. 205-221. London: Academic Press.

1987 Women and Health Care on a Guatemalan Plantation. Social Science and Medicine 25(10):1163-1173.

Cosminsky, Sheila and Ira Harrison

1984 Traditional Medicine: Implications for Ethnomedicine, Ethno-pharmacology, Maternal and Child Health, and Public Health. An Annotated Bibliography of Africa, Latin America, and the Carribean. Vol. II. New York: Garland. (for Vol. I, see Harrison and Cosminsky 1976).

Cosminsky, Sheila and Mary Scrimshaw

1980 Medical Pluralism on a Guatemalan Plantation. Social Science and Medicine 14B(4):267-278.

Cruz, J. R., et al.

1990 Epidemiology of Acute Respiratory Tract Infections among Guatemalan Ambulatory Preschool Children. Review of Infectious Diseases 12 suppl. 8:S1029-1034.

Davis, Shelton H. and Julie Hodson

1982 Witness to Political Violence in Guatemala: The Suppression of a Rural Development Program. Boston: Oxfam America.

Delgado, H. L., et al.

1988 Epidemiology of Acute Respiratory Infections in Preschool Children of Rural Guatemala. PAHO Bulletin 22(4):383-393.

Early, John D.

1982 The Demographic Structure and Evolution of a Peasant System: The Guatemalan Population. Boca Raton: University of Florida.

Edmunson, Munro S. (trans.)

1971 The Book of Counsel: The Popol Vuh of the Quiché Maya of Guatemala. Middle American Research Institute, Publication 35. New Orleans: Tulane University Press.

Falla, Ricardo

1983 The Massacre at the Rural Estate of San Francisco 1982. Cultural Survival 7(1):43-45.

Fauriol, Georges A. and Eva Loser

1991 Guatemala's Political Puzzle. Washington D.C.: Center for Strategic and International Affairs.

Fielder, John L.

1985 Health Policy and Additive Reform: The Case of Guatemala. International Journal of Health Services 15:275-299.

Flores, Marina.
1976 Food Attitudes to Actualize Community Nutrition Education. In: Nutrition and Agricultural Development. Nevin Scrimshaw and M. Behar (eds.). Pp. 275-287. New York: The Plenum Press.

Flores, Marina, Zoila Flores, and Marta Lara
1966 Food Intake of Guatemalan Children, ages 1-5. Journal of the American Dietetic Association. June 1966:400-487.

Gillin, John P.
1948 Magical Fright. Psychiatry 11:387-408.
1951 The Culture of Security in San Carlos: A Study of a Guatemalan Community of Indians and Ladinos. Middle American Research Institute, Publication 16. New Orleans: Tulane University Press.
1956 The Making of a Witch Doctor. Psychiatry 19(2):131-136.

Goldin, L.
1991 An Expression of Cultural Change: Invisible Converts to Protestantism Among Highland Guatemalan Mayas. Ethnology 30(4):325-328.
1992 Work and Ideology in the Maya Highland of Guatemala: Economic Beliefs in the Context of Occupational Change. Economic Development and Cultural Change 41(1):103-112.

Gonzalez, Nancie S.
1964 Beliefs and Practices Concerning Medicine and Nutrition among Lower-Class Urban Guatemalans. American Journal of Public Health 54(10):1726-1734.
1966 Health Behavior in Cross-Cultural Perspective: A Guatemalan Example. Human Organization 25:122-125.

Green, Linda Buckley
1989 Consensus and Coercion: Primary Health Care and the Guatemalan State. Medical Anthropology Quarterly 3:246-257.

Greenburg, L.
1982 Midwife Training Programs in Highland Guatemala. Social Science and Medicine 16(18):1599-1609.

Harrison, Ira and Sheila Cosminsky
1976 Traditional Medicine: Implications for Ethnomedicine, Ethno-pharmacology, Maternal and Child Health, and Public Health. An annotated Bibliography of Africa, Latin America, and the Carribean. Vol. I. New York: Garland. (for Vol. II, see Cosminsky and Harrison, 1984).

Hawkins, John
  1984 Inverse Images: The Meaning of Culture, Ethnicity, and Family in Post-Colonial Guatemala. Albuquerque: University of New Mexico Press.
Hearst, Norman
  1985 Infant Mortality in Guatemala: An Epidemiological Perspective. International Journal of Epidemiology 14:575-581.
Hinshaw, Robert
  1975 Panajachel: A Guatemalan Town in Thirty Year Perspective. Pittsburg: University of Pittsburg Press.
Instituto de Nutrición de Centro America y Panama (INCAP)
  1990 Guatemala 1987: Results from the Demographic and Health Survey. Studies in Family Planning 21(1):55-59.
Johnston, Francis E., et al.
  1989 Socioeconomic Correlates of Fertility, Mortality, and Child Survival in Mothers from a Disadvantaged, Urban Guatemalan Community. American Journal of Human Biology 1:25-30.
Kelsey, Vera and Lilly de Jongh Osborne
  1951 Four Keys to Guatemala. New York: Wilfred Funk.
King, Arden R.
  1974 Coban and Verapaz: History and Cultural Process in Northern Guatemala. New Orleans: Tulane University Press.
La Farge, Oliver
  1940 Maya Ethnology: The Sequence of Cultures. In: C.L. Hay et al (eds.), The Maya and their Neighbors. Pp. 281-291. New York: Appleton-Century.
  1947 Santa Eulalia. Chicago: University of Chicago Press.
La Farge, Oliver and Douglas Byers
  1931 The Year Bearer's People. Middle American Research Institute, Publication 3. New Orleans: Tulane University Press.
Logan, Michael H.
  1973a Digestive Disorders and Plant Medicinals in Highland Guatemala. Anthropos 68:537-547.
  1973b Humoral Medicine in Guatemala and Peasant Acceptance of Modern Medicine. Human Organization 32(4):385-395.
  1979 Variations Regarding Susto Causality Among the Cakchiquel of Guatemala. Culture, Medicine and Psychiatry 3:153-166.
Logan, Michael H. and Warren T. Morrill
  1979 Humoral Medicine and Informant Variability: An Analysis of Acculturation and Cognitive Change among Guatemalan Villagers. Anthropos 74:784-802.

Logan, Michael H. and Hector N. Qirko
   1990 Ladinoization in Guatemala: A Darwinian Perspective. SECOLAS Annals 21:89-98.
Manz, Beatriz
   1988 Refugees of a Hidden War: The Aftermath of Counterinsurgency in Guatemala. Albany: State University of New York Press.
Mata, Leonardo
   1978 The Children of Santa María Cauque: A Prospective Field Study of Health and Growth. Cambridge: MIT Press.
   1980 Child Malnutrition and Deprivation in Guatemala and Costa Rica. Food and Nutrition (Roma) 6(2):7-14.
Mathewson, Kent
   1984 Irrigation Horticulture in Highland Guatemala: The Tablón System of Panajachel. Boulder: Westview Press.
McBryde, Felix W.
   1933 Sololá: A Guatemalan Town and Cakchiquel Market Center. Middle American Research Institute, Publication 5:45-152. New Orleans: Tulane University Press.
   1947 Cultural and Historical Geography of Southwestern Guatemala. Washington, D.C.: Smithsonian Institution, Institute of Social Anthropology, Publication 4.
McGlynn, Eileen A.
   1975 Middle American Anthropology: Directory, Bibliography, and Guide to the UCLA Library Collections. Los Angeles: University of California Press.
Mellon, G.
   1974 El Uso de las Plantas Medicinales en Guatemala. Guatemala Indígena 9(1-2):99-179.
Melville, Margery
   1971 Guatemala Vietnam? Penguin Books Limited.
Melville, M. B. and M. B. Lykes
   1992 Guatemalan Indian Children and the Sociocultural Effects of Government-Sponsored Terrorism. Social Science and Medicine 34(5):533-548.
Mendez Dominquez, Alfredo
   1983 Illness and Medical Theory among the Guatemalan Indians. In: Heritage of Conquest: Thirty Years Later. C. Kendall, J. Hawkins, and L. Bossen (eds.). Pp. 267-298. Albuquerque: University of New Mexico Press.

Moore, G. Alexander
  1973 Life Cycles of Atchalán: The Diverse Careers of Certain Guate-
        malans. New York: Teacher's College Press.
Moors, Marilyn (ed.)
  1990 Guatemalan Indians and the State, 1540-1988. Austin: University
        of Texas Press.
Nash, Manning
  1969 Guatemalan Highlands. In: Handbook of Middle American
        Indians, vol. 7: Ethnology; section 1: The Maya. E. Vogt (vol.
        ed.). Pp. 30-45. R. Wauchope (general ed.). Austin: University
        of Texas Press.
Neuenswander, Helen and Shirley Souder
  1977 The Hot-Cold Wet-Dry Syndrome among the Quiche of Joyabaj:
        Two Alternative Cognitive Models. In Cognitive Studies of
        Southern Mesoamerica, Helen Neuenswander and Dean Arnold
        (eds.) Pp. 93-125. Dallas: Summer Institute of Linguistics,
        Museum of Anthropology.
Oakes, Maud
  1951 Two Crosses of Todos Santos. New York: Pantheon Books.
Orellana, Sandra L.
  1977 Aboriginal Medicine in Highland Guatemala.   Medical
        Anthropology 1(5):114-156.
  1981 Idols and Idolatry in Highland Guatemala.   Ethnohistory
        28:157-177.
  1987 Indian Medicine in Highland Guatemala: The Pre-Hispanic and
        Colonial Periods. Albuquerque: University of New Mexico
        Press.
Osborne, Lilly de Jongh
  1965 Indian Crafts of Guatemala and El Salvador.   Norman:
        University of Oklahoma Press.
Paul, Benjamin D.
  1976 The Maya Bonesetter as Sacred Specialist. Ethnology 15(1):77-81.
Paul, Lois
  1975 Recruitment to a Ritual Role: The Midwife in a Maya
        Community. Ethnos 3(3):449-467.
Paul, Lois and Benjamin D. Paul
  1975 The Maya Midwife as Sacred Specialist: A Guatemalan Case.
        American Ethnologist 2:707-726. Adrián Recinos, Delia Goetz,
        and Dionisio José Chonay (trans. and eds.).
  1953 The Annals of the Cakchiquels and Title of the Lords of
        Totonicapán. Norman: University of Oklahoma Press.

Reina, Ruben
  1966 Law of the Saints: A Pokomam Pueblo and its Community
       Culture. Indianapolis: Bobbs-Merrill Publishing.
  1969 Eastern Guatemalan Highlands: The Pokomames and Chorti.
       In: Handbook of Middle American Indians, vol. 7: Ethnology;
       section 1: The Maya. E. Vogt (vol. ed.). Pp. 333-355. R.
       Wauchope (general ed.). Austin: University of Texas Press.
Reina, Ruben and Robert M. Hill
  1978 The Traditional Pottery of Guatemala. Austin: University of
       Texas Press.
Rodman, Selden
  1967 The Guatemala Traveler. New York: Meredith Press.
Rodriquez Rouanet, Francisco
  1971 Aspectos de la Medicina Popular en el Área Rural de
       Guatemala. Guatemala Indigena 6(1):1-330.
Ronstrom, Anitha
  1989 Children in Central America: Victims of War. Child Welfare
       68(2):145-153.
Rowe, Ann P.
  1981 A Century of Change in Guatemalan Textiles. Seattle:
       University of Washington Press.
Roys, Ralph L.
  1931 The Ethno-Botany of the Maya. Middle American Research
       Institute, Publication 2. New Orleans: Tulane University.
Saler, B.
  1964 Nagual, Witch, and Sorcerer in a Quiché Village. Ethnology
       3:305-327.
Salomon, J. B., Leonardo Mata, and J. Gordon
  1968 Malnutrition and the Communicable Diseases of Childhood in
       Rural Guatemala. American Journal of Public Health 58:505-516.
Sauvain-Dugerdil, Claudine
  1981 Bio-Anthropology in San Antonio Palopo. In: Mayan Studies:
       The Midwestern Highlands of Guatemala. J. Loucky and M.
       Hurwicz (eds.). Pp. 101-117. Anthropology UCLA, vol. 11, nos.
       1 and 2.
Schwartz, Norman B.
  1977 A Milpero of Petén, Guatemala: Autobiography and Cultural
       Analysis. Newark: University of Delaware Latin American
       Studies Program.

Scrimshaw, Nevin S.
1970 Synergism of Malnutrition and Infection: Evidence from Field
      Studies in Guatemala. Journal of the American Medical
      Association 212:1685-1692.
Scrimshaw, Nevin S. and C. Tejada
1970 Pathology of Living Indians as Seen in Guatemala. In:
      Handbook of Middle American Indians, vol. 9. T.D. Stewart
      (vol. ed.). Pp. 203-225. R. Wauchope (general ed.). Austin:
      University of Texas Press.
Scrimshaw, Nevin S., et al.
1968 Nutrition and Infection Field Study in Guatemalan Villages,
      1959-1964. Archives of Environmental Health 16:223-234.
Sexton, James D.
1979 Education and Acculturation in Highland Guatemala. Anthro-
      pology and Education Quarterly 10(2):80-95.
Sexton, James D. (ed.)
1981 Son of Tecún Umán: A Maya Indian Tells His Story. Prospect
      Heights, IL.: Waveland Press.
1985 Campesino: The Diary of a Guatemalan Indian. Tucson:
      University of Arizona Press.
Sexton, James D. and Clyde M. Woods
1977 Development and Modernization among Highland Maya: A
      Comparative Analysis of Ten Guatemalan Towns. Human
      Organization 36(2):156-172.
Shattuck, George C. (ed.)
1938 A Medical Survey of Guatemala. Washington, D. C.: Carnegie
      Institute.
Simeon, George
1973 The Evil Eye in a Guatemalan Village. Ethnomedizin 2(3/4):
      437-441.
Sindell, P. and J. Tenzel
1970 Shamanism and Concepts of Disease in a Mayan Indian
      Community. Transcultural Psychiatric Research Review
      7:188-190.
Smith, C.A.(ed.)
1990 Guatemalan Indians and the State, 1540-1988. Austin: University
      of Texas Press.
Smith, Waldemar R.
1978 The Fiesta System and Economic Change. New York: Columbia
      University Press.

Sperlich, Norbert and Elizabeth Katz Sperlich
    1980 Guatemalan Backstrap Weaving.   Norman: University of
        Oklahoma Press.
Standley, Paul C. and Julian A. Steyermark
    1946-52 Flora of Guatemala. Fieldiana: Botany. Chicago: Field Museum
        of Natural History.
Standley, Paul C. and L. O. Williams
    1961-73 Flora of Guatemala. Fieldiana: Botany. Chicago: Field
        Museum of Natural History.
Tax, Sol
    1937 The Municipios of the Midwestern Highlands of Guatemala.
        American Anthropologist 39:423-444.
    1953 Penny Capitalism: A Guatemalan Indian Economy. Washington,
        D.C.: Smithsonian Institution, Institute of Social Anthropology,
        Publication 16.
Tax, Sol (ed.)
    1952 Heritage of Conquest. Glencoe, Illinois: The Free Press.
Tax, Sol and Robert Hinshaw
    1969 The Maya of the Midwestern Highlands. In: Handbook of
        Middle American Indians, vol. 7: Ethnology; section 1: The
        Maya. E. Vogt (vol. ed.). Pp. 333-355. R. Wauchope (general
        ed.). Austin: University of Texas Press.
Tedlock, Barbara
    1982 Time and the Highland Maya. Albuquerque: University of New
        Mexico Press.
Tenzel, J. H.
    1970 Shamanism and Concepts of Disease in a Mayan Indian
        Community. Psychiatry 33:372-380.
Thompson, J. Eric S.
    1970 Maya History and Religion. Norman: University of Oklahoma
        Press.
Torun, Benjamin
    1983 Environmental and Educational Interventions against Diarrhea
        in Guatemala. In: Diarrhea and Malnutrition: Interactions,
        Mechanisms, and Interventions. L. C. Chen and N. S.
        Scrimshaw (eds.). New York: Plenum Press.
Valle, Rafael H.
    1971 Bibliografía Maya. New York: Burt Franklin.

Wagley, Charles
   1941   Economics of a Guatemalan Village. American Anthropological
          Association Memoirs, no. 58.
   1969   The Maya of Northwestern Guatemala. In: Handbook of
          Middle American Indians, vol. 7: Ethnology; section 1: The
          Maya. E. Vogt (vol. ed.). Pp. 333-355. R. Wauchope (general
          ed.). Austin: University of Texas Press.
Warren, Kay B.
   1978   The Symbolism of Subordination: Indian Identity in a
          Guatemalan Town. Austin: University of Texas Press.
Weller, Susan C.
   1983   New Data on Intracultural Variability: The Hot-Cold Concept
          of Medicine and Illness. Human Organization 42:249-257.
   1984   Cross-Cultural Concepts of Illness: Variation and Validation.
          American Anthropologist 86:341-351.
Weller, Susan C., Trenton K. Ruebush, and Robert E. Klein
   1991   An Epidemiological Description of a Folk Illness: A Study of
          Empacho in Guatemala. Medical Anthropology 13(1-2):19-31.
Whetten, Nathan L.
   1961   Guatemala: Its Land and Its People. New Haven: Yale
          University Press.
Williams, L. O.
   1981   The Useful Plants of Central America. Ceiba 24:10-237.
Wisdom, Charles
   1940   The Chorti Indians of Guatemala. Chicago: University of
          Chicago Press.
Woods, Clyde M.
   1977   Curing Strategies in a Changing Medical Situation. Medical
          Anthropology 3:26-54.
Woods, Clyde and Theodore Graves
   1973   The Process of Medical Change in a Highland Guatemalan
          Town. Los Angeles: Latin American Center, University of
          California at Los Angeles.

TOWARD WORLDWIDE PRIMARY HEALTH CARE

These selected titles indicate how practices and studies in Guatemala have entered into the broader discussion of "health for all," cite recent landmarks of world agreement, and point to the terms and issues in controversy.

Beauchamp, Dan
  1976 Public Health as Social Justice. Inquiry 13:3-14.
Chave, S.P.W.
  1984 The Origins and Development of Public Health. In: Oxford Textbook of Public Health. Vol I: History, Determinants, Scope, and Strategies. W.W. Holland, R. Detels, and G. Knox (eds.). New York: Oxford University Press.
Committee for the Study of the Future of Public Health
  1988 The Future of Public Health. Project of the Institute of Medicine, the National Academy of Sciences. Washington, DC: National Academy Press.
Ellencweig, Avi Yacar and Ruthellen B. Yoshpe
  1984 Definition of Public Health. Public Health Review 12:65-78.
Goudsblom, Johan
  1986 Public Health and the Civilizing Process. The Milbank Quarterly 64(2):161-88.
Habicht, Jean-Pierre
  1979 Assurance of Quality in the Provision of Primary Medical Care by Non-Professionals. Social Science and Medicine 13B:67-75.
Heggenhougen, H. K.
  1984 Will Primary Health Care Efforts be Allowed to Succeed? Social Science and Medicine 19(3):217-24.
Heggenhougen, H.K. and Alizon Draper
  1990 Medical Anthropology and Primary Health Care: An Introduction and Selected Annotated Bibliography. London: Evaluation and Planning Centre for Health Care, London School of Hygiene and Tropical Medicine.
Hope, Anne and Sally Timmel
  1984 Training for Transformation: A Handbook for Community Workers. 3 vols. Published in Spanish and English. Gweru, Zimbabwe: Mambo Press.

Illich, Ivan
  1973   Two Watersheds. In: Tools for Conviviality. Pp. 1-9. New York: Harper.
  1976   Medical Nemesis: The Expropriation of Health. New York: Pantheon.
Mahler, Halfdan
  1988   Social Justice—The Underpinning for Health Leadership Development. Ira Hiscock Public Lecture at the University of Hawaii School of Public Health. In: The Congressional Record—Senate, October 17, 1988. S1604-7.
Moore, Lorna, Peter Van Arsdale, JoAnn Glittenberg and Robert Aldrich
  1980   The Biocultural Basis of Health. Prospect Heights, IL: Waveland Press. Reissued 1987 with changes.
Pan-American Health Organization
  1986   Health Conditions in the Americas 1981-1984. Vol. 2. Washington, D.C.: PAHO.
  1990   Guatemala Health Conditions in the Americas. 1990 ed., Vol. 2. Washington, D. C.: PAHO.
  1992   The Crisis of Public Health: Reflections for the Debate. Scientific Publication No. 540. Washington D.C.: PAHO.
Roemer, Milton I.
  1991   National Health Systems of the World, vol. 1 (see Guatemala, pp. 357-362). New York: Oxford University Press.
Starr, Paul
  1982   The Social Transformation of American Medicine. New York: Basic Books.
Terris, Milton
  1972   The Epidemiologic Revolution. American Journal of Public Health 62:11 (November):1439-41.
Werner, David
  1977   Where there is no Doctor. First English ed. Palo Alto: Hesperian Foundation.
World Health Organization
  1978   Alma-Ata Declaration: Primary Health Care.
  1979   Formulating Strategies for Health for All by the Year 2000.
  1981   Global Strategy for Health for All by the Year 2000.
         Development of Indicators for Monitoring Progress towards Health for All by the Year 2000.
         Managerial Process for National Health Development: Guiding Principles.
         Health Programme Evaluation: Guiding Principles.

1982   Plan of Action for Implementing the Global Strategy for Health for All, with Index to the Series.
       Seventh General Programme of Work covering the Period 1984-89.
1984   Glossary of Terms used in the Series.
1987   Eighth General Programme of Work covering the Period 1990-95.
       In: "Health For All Series." Geneva, Switzerland: Office of Publications.

CONTRIBUTORS

CARROLL BEHRHORST, MD, was founder and coordinator of the Chimaltenango Development Program in Guatemala. After medical school at Washington University in St. Louis, internships in Cleveland and St. Louis, and service as a medical officer with the U.S. Navy, he conducted a family medical practice in Winfield, Kansas (1951-58). In 1960, pursuing an earlier vision, he closed this practice and moved with his family to Guatemala under auspices of a Lutheran church body. Two years later he moved independently to Chimaltenango in the highlands where he opened a house clinic and later built a hospital with the Kaqchikel-Maya.

The work grew to include health promoters, health and nutrition education, potable water projects, agricultural extension, credit and land acquisition—always undertaken in cooperation with village leaders and in conjunction with community organization. The program gained worldwide recognition for its response during the earthquakes of 1976. In the years following, it was cited by the World Health Organization as a model of health promotion and was consulted in the planning of primary health strategies on several continents. During the violence which focused on Chimaltenango during the early 1980s, the clinic remained open to the people and casualties on both sides. The doctor removed his family from the country briefly after a brutal episode affecting relatives of his wife, Alicia.

From 1982 Behrhorst also served as an adjunct professor working with international and other students in the Tulane University School of Public Health and Tropical Medicine. His contributions have been acknowledged by doctorates from six universities and by major awards of medical and health associations. He married twice and fathered ten children, six born to Elizabeth (nee) King and four to Alicia Nicolás (one of these by a previous marriage). He died in 1990 and was buried at Chimazat in the Department of Chimaltenango.

JUANITA BATZIBAL TUJAL is president of the International Mayan League, now working in Costa Rica. A native of Patzún, Chimaltenango, she has known the Behrhorst foundation from its beginnings, especially the work of extensionists and nurses from her village. The conversation reproduced in this book took place during a visit to Chicago in 1991, which included seminars on the *Pop Wuj*, sacred book of the Quiché Maya.

RALPH CRAWSHAW, MD, Portland, Oregon, is a board member of Health Volunteers Overseas which places physicians from North America along side indigenous workers in other countries, a leader of Oregon Health Decisions and American Health Decisions which foster citizen initiatives in health planning and policy, and a member of the National Academy of Science, Institute of Medicine. He founded The Club of KOS for Health Care, whose newsletter featured a program report by Behrhorst in June, 1978, and his own report of a visit to Chimaltenango in April, 1986.

ISSAKHA DIALLO, MPH, Director, Department of Primary Health Care in the Senegalese Ministry of Health, studied with Behrhorst in the Tulane University School of Public Health and Tropical Medicine, preparing for work in his native country. He is now a teacher in the Institute for Health and Development at the University of Cheikh Anta Diop in Dakar, a program which cooperates with the Tulane school and Morehouse Medical School.

WILLIAM H. FOEGE, MD, MPH, is Executive Director, the Carter Center of Emory University and Global 2000 of the Carter Presidential Center, Inc. After serving as a medical missionary in Nigeria and as an epidemiologist in the successful campaign to eradicate smallpox during the 1970s, he became director of the Centers for Disease Control. He helped form the Task Force for Child Survival, a working group including the World Health Organization, United Nations Children's Fund, the World Bank, the United Nations Development Program, and the Rockefeller Foundation, and has served as President of the American Public Health Association. Global 2000 projects are assisting communities to become self-sufficient by combating the crippling diseases of Guinea worm and River Blindness and teaching basic agricultural practices.

WAYNE L. HAAG, PHD, is director of the Sasakawa Global 2000 program in Ghana, West Africa. After living and working in Guatemalan villages with the Behrhorst program as a Peace Corps volunteer and as staff of World Neighbors, he did advanced work in crop science in Costa Rica with the Interamerican Institute of Agricultural Sciences, a project of the Organization of American States. His doctoral studies in agronomy included work in India and his post-doctoral work with the International Center for Maize and Wheat Improvement was done in Mexico, Egypt, Turkey and Colombia. The work in Ghana includes developing and promoting the use of quality protein maize.

H. KRIS HEGGENHOUGEN, PHD, is Associate Professor in the Department of Social Medicine of the Harvard Medical School, and in the Department of Population Sciences and International Health of the Harvard School of Public Health. Work in Latin America during the early 1970s included a year and a half with the Behrhorst program, living in the village of Simajuleu (Kaqchikel, "Edge of the World"), which became the subject of his dissertation entitled *Health Care at the Edge of the World* (New School of Social Research, 1976). This writer spent the 1980s with the Evaluation and Planning Centre of the London School of Hygiene and Tropical Medicine, working for three years in Malaysia and three years in Tanzania.

JONATHAN HORTON, MD, PHD, is a specialist on neurovisual disorders in the Medical School, University of California, San Francisco. He served as physician's assistant in Chimaltenango from February to June, 1984, and is married to Lidia Mucia, who worked for twelve years as a nurse of the clinic in Chimaltenango.

MICHAEL H. LOGAN, PHD, Associate Professor of Anthropology, University of Tennessee, has studied medical beliefs and practices in the American southwest, Mexico, Brazil and Guatemala. His publications include studies of fright-sickness and humoral theories of disease. All royalties earned from the sale of a book co-edited with E. E. Hunt, *Health and the Human Condition: Perspectives on Medical Anthropology* (1978), were donated to the Behrhorst programs in Chimaltenango.

RICHARD LUECKE, PHD, Community Renewal Society, Chicago, is a pastor and philosophy teacher who has cooperated with central city communities in seeking social and economic stability and in training organizers, leaders and clergy. He has conducted city-wide studies and programs on work and health. He is a board member of the International Mayan League and of the Behrhorst Clinic Foundation in North America.

HALFDAN MAHLER, MD, Director General emeritus of the World Health Organization and Secretary General of International Planned Parenthood Federation, is a world educator in concepts and strategies of primary health care.

ANTONIO MARTÍNEZ, PHD, is director of the Kovler Center for the Treatment of Survivors of Torture, a project of Travellers and Immigrants Aid in Chicago, and a board member of the International Mayan League.

JOHN MCKNIGHT, Center for Urban Affairs and Policy Research, Northwestern University, was a participant with Carroll Behrhorst in consultations on alternatives in health care convened in Cuernavaca, Mexico, during the 1970s. He is an international exponent of community development based on capacities rather than needs and cooperation rather than competition.

CHRISTOPHER MURRILL is a graduate student in public health at Tulane University School of Public Health and Tropical Medicine. At the time of this writing he was on assignment in Senegal coordinating a rural field study of traditional healers.

MARIO NOJ, General Secretary of the International Maya League, is a native of Chimaltenango who now works in theology and Mayan studies in Costa Rica.

PATRICIA O'CONNOR, PHD, is a Health, Population and Nutrition Officer of the United States Agency for International Development, who has worked with communities in Bolivia, Costa Rica, Guatemala and Tanzania on problems of AIDS, malaria, family planning and nutrition. Since her work as a graduate student with the Chimaltenango program, she has prepared evaluation instruments, training designs and reports of its work, and is a board member of the Behrhorst foundation in North America.

MARÍA HORTENSIA OTZOY DE CAP is a native of San Juan Comalapa, Chimaltenango, who began work in 1964 with Behrhorst programs of health education and agriculture in the villages. These included five years as a health promoter under the auspices of World Neighbors. In 1981 she became a nurse in the Behrhorst hospital and in 1989 acquired a certificate in nursing from the Guatemalan Ministry of Health. She is a founder of Nuevo Amanecer, an organization of indigenous workers in the program.

NIGEL PANETH, MD, MPH, is Director of the Program in Epidemiology and Professor of Pediatrics at Michigan State University. During 1972 he worked with the Central American Institute of Nutrition (INCAP) as a student in tropical medicine at San Martín Jilotopeque in the Guatemalan highlands, where he met Behrhorst and cooperated with Chimaltenango programs.

ROBERT PATRICK is a graduate student in anthropology at the university of Tennessee in Knoxville, whose work is focused on illness control beliefs of people in Appalachia and Brazil.

JOHN PUELLE is treasurer of the Behrhorst foundation in North America and has served as a liason between the boards north and south. He previously worked as a pastor and linguist in Guatemala.

VICTOR W. SIDEL, MD, is Distinguished University Professor of Social Medicine, Montefiore Medical Center, Albert Einstein College of Medicine. Along with extensive work in community health, especially in the Bronx, New York, he has served with medical study commissions including the Physician Task Force on Hunger in America and the U.S. medical delegation invited to China in 1971. Subsequent visits to that country resulted in two books and many articles on health care in China. He was a representative to Oslo for the 1985 Nobel Prize to International Physicians for the Prevention of Nuclear War. He is a past president of Physicians for Social Responsibility, the Public Health Association of New York City and the American Public Health Association.

ULLI STELTZER is a social photographer whose collections at Princeton University and nine books include studies of peoples of the southwestern United States, the west coast of Canada and the Inuit as well as of highland Guatemala. Her *Health in the Guatemalan Highlands* (1983) includes a description of the Chimaltenango project by Carroll Behrhorst and expressions by Mayan workers.

BRIAN LEO TREACY is an attorney who has served as a legal protection officer in Central America, Tanzania and Kenya for the United Nations High Commissioner for Refugees. He has also worked with refugees to the United States from Latin America and Southeast Asia. He is a member of the board of the Behrhorst Clinic Foundation, Inc., in North America.

FELIPA XICO AJQUEJAY is a native of Patzicía, Chimaltenango, who serves as a health educator and a vice-president of the foundation in Guatemala. During more than 20 years with the program she has pursued a degree in social work and has also cooperated with the Guatemalan Ministry of Urban and Rural Development and with international aid organizations. She is a founder and leading spirit of Nuevo Amanecer, devoted to maintaining the philosophy and indigenous character of the Chimaltenango programs.

CARLOS XOQUIC CAY is president of the Fundación Guatemalteca para el Desarrollo "Carroll Behrhorst." He began work as a health promoter in the early years of the program and served as coordinator of the promoters. He is also president of FECOMERC, a farmers' cooperative, which was formed with the assistance of the foundation.